The OXFORDSHIRE *Cook Book*

A celebration of the amazing food & drink on our doorstep.
Featuring over 45 stunning recipes.

FOREWORD

Chef Mike North has held a Michelin star at The Nut Tree Inn for the last eight years and believes that Oxford's gastronomy has so much to offer, from nationally acclaimed artisan bakers and delicatessens to amazing local butchers...

Firstly, I am a chef, not a writer, therefore please forgive me if this is a little amateurish. What I will say is that it's an absolute pleasure and honour to be asked to write this foreword.

My roots lie here in Oxfordshire. My mother's side of the family are from central Oxford, my grandfather was a professor at Oxford University and my grandmother was also involved in Oxford's esteemed academia.

My paternal grandparents were involved in farming and butchery with their roots lying firmly where we are now, in the beautiful and historic villages of Otmoor, about 10 miles north of Oxford's dreaming spires.

Being one of eight children, my mother spent a lot of time in the kitchen, which is where my passion for cooking began.

Oxford's gastronomy has so much to offer, from nationally acclaimed artisan bakers and delicatessens to amazing local butchers such as Gabriel Machin in Henley-on-Thames, independent wine merchants such as Eynsham Cellars, celebrated cheese shop The Oxford Cheese Company, a plethora of farm shops who bring the freshest local produce together and local producers making everything from cakes to chocolates.

If you're out eating the choice is immense, from cosy country pubs like The Nut Tree Inn, to the vibrant bistros and cool cafés of Oxford. The local food heroes of Oxfordshire are too many to mention, but in short, I am sure you will find in this book a place to suit you for every occasion and every budget.

Enjoy.

Mike North

The Oxfordshire Cook Book

©2016 Meze Publishing. All rights reserved.

First edition printed in 2016 in the UK.

ISBN: 978-1-910863-08-4

Thank you to: Mike North at The Nut Tree Inn, Christine Wallace, Kat Orman

Compiled by: Heather Hawkins

Written by: Kate Eddison, Rachel Heward

Photography by:

Sam Bowles (www.portraitcollective.com)
Paul Carroll (www.portraitcollective.com)
Robbie Stephenson (www.portraitcollective.com)

Edited by: Rachel Heward, Phil Turner

Designed by: Paul Cocker, Marc Barker

Cover art: Luke Prest (www.lukeprest.com)

Contributors: Faye Bailey, Kerre Chen, Holly Vincent

Printed by Bell and Bain Ltd, Glasgow

Published by Meze Publishing Limited
Unit 1 Beehive Works
Milton Street
Sheffield S3 7WL
Web: www.mezepublishing.co.uk
Tel: 0114 275 7709
Email: info@mezepublishing.co.uk

CONTENTS

Meet the
WINE EXPERTS

An independent wine shop in the centre of Eynsham, Eynsham Cellars has been helping local wine-lovers choose the perfect bottle since 2010.

Having worked in different wine shops for many years, Oli and Iain had only been working together for 6 weeks when the large wine retailer they worked for announced they were being made redundant. They had both been dreaming of opening their own independent wine shop, eager to be able to have control over the wines they sold with no restraints – so they decided to see this as a serendipitous opportunity and start their own business together.

They chose to re-open a High Street shop that Oli was familiar with in the heart of Eynsham, a thriving village with a growing collection of independent food shops. The enthusiastic pair had no doubt that they could offer something a bit different to the community. The shop is welcoming with a relaxed feel about it. They aim to break down any barriers that can make specialist wine shops feel a bit intimidating for people and are always happy to offer advice, whether it's choosing a special gift, wine to match food at a dinner party or just something to enjoy with a pizza.

The small store is packed with over 400 different wines from all around the world, not to mention more than 60 bottled ales and some fine spirits, too. Limited only by how many they can fit on the shelves, Oli and Iain regularly visit trade shows across the country and embark on epic tasting days meeting suppliers from around the world to select products.

And neither Oli nor Iain can remember the last time they went on holiday and didn't squeeze in a trip to a vineyard!

They love to be able to source bottles for customers, and have built up relationships with their regulars, many of whom they know by name and trust them to recommend new discoveries. They have become a key part of the Eynsham community, hosting tasting days and occasional pop-up events with their neighbours at Cornucopia.

Matching wine and food is a skill that is daunting for most people, and never more so than when hosting a large event or wedding. Eynsham Cellars offer an outstanding wedding service, where they supply the wine and glass hire, and throw in a completely stress-free service to go with it. Sit down with Iain and Oli for a private tasting and they'll help you select the perfect wines to match your meal at the right budget. With so many satisfied customers already raving about their knowledge and service, it's clear you couldn't put your wine selection in safer hands.

The wine MATCHING

Oli and Iain at Eynsham Cellars have recommended the following wines and beers to go alongside the recipes in this book, ensuring you'll always have the perfect accompaniment. They are all available from their shop in Eynsham, or online at www.eynshamcellars.com.

THE BASKERVILLE
Bouillabaisse
Domaine Laguilhon Jurançon Sec 2013 £13
Slightly aromatic and a little tropical, but with fresh crisp pear flavours, this beauty from south west France will pair wonderfully with this gently-spiced fish stew.

CHADLINGTON QUALITY FOODS
Salmon & broccoli pie
Domain Perraud Macon-Villages Chardonnay 2014 £13
The creamy, salmon pie paired with this gently-oaked, slightly buttery and quite fruity White Burgundy should put a smile on your face.

CHADLINGTON QUALITY FOODS
Apricot & almond tart
Graham Beck 'Bliss' Western Cape Demi-Sec Sparkling £14
Sparkling wine is usually used as an aperitif in the UK, but this South African traditional method 'demi sec' (actually really quite sweet) fizz will pair excellently with this apricot and almond tart.

THE CHERRY TREE INN
Woodland mushroom, white truffle and wild garlic flatbreads & potted rabbit rillettes
Fattoria Selvapiana, Chianti Rufina DOCG 2013 £14
A slightly gamier style of Chianti, exactly what this rich rabbit, Chianti and mushroom dish calls out for. Just make sure you still have plenty to drink if you use it in the rillettes!

CHRISTINE WALLACE
St Clements dreamy layer cake
Langlois-Chateau Coteaux du Layon, Loire 2012 (375ml) £12
This St Clements layer cake calls for a pudding wine which is not overly viscous, with lots of citrus flavours. This classic Loire Chenin, full of orange blossom and honey flavours will work a treat. Delicious!

COTSWOLD BAKING
Rhubarb & almond streusel tart
Domaine Laguilhon Jurançon 2012 £14.50
This wine from south west France, laden with almond and apricot flavours, this will complement the pudding perfectly.

THE CROOKED BILLET
Rack of goat, shepherd's pie
Montes Tosacanini 'Criado en Roble' Blend Tinto, Las Piedras Canelones (Uruguay) 2012 £18
A blend based around Uruguay's signature (and in some circles thought to be very healthy) Tannat variety, this big, hearty red will be wonderful alongside this spiced goat shepherd's pie.

THE CROOKED BILLET

Builders tea brûlée, milk chocolate hob nobs

Vito Curatolo Arini Marsala Dolce £13.50

If you choose not to go with tea, why not have a quality sweet Sicilian Marsala? The biscuits will also be amazing dipped in the glass as the Italians do. Standard operating procedure we promise.

COGGES KITCHEN

Kelmscott bacon and cheddar muffins

Gordon & Mcphail Connoisseurs Choice Caol Ila 2003 £46

Cancel your appointments and savour a wee dram of peat filled smoky, salty, bacon flavoured Islay single malt – it will be stunning with these tasty muffins. Just make sure if they are for breakfast that you don't have anything else to do! Alternatively try the Rauk smoke beer from Church Hanbrewery.

DELICACY

Maftoul rose salad

Cave Hunawihr 'Reserve' Alsace Gewurztraminer 2014 £14

The rose and pomegranate in this salad will be perfectly matched by the aroma of this Alsace Gewurz, and the tiniest hint of sweetness in the wine will complement the spice and molasses.

FINGERS AND FORKS

Spicy sesame tuna tartare with wasabi cream

Kung Fu Girl Riesling 2014 £14:

Try this kick-ass, almost dry Riesling made by ex-rock band manager Charles Smith in Washington State. Fresh and fruity with hints of lime, it's just aromatic enough for this spicy tuna.

GABRIEL MACHIN

Beef carbonnade with Henley Dark Ale and horseradish dumplings

Les Cepages Oublies Mourvèdre 2013 £8.50

This hearty dish calls for a dark and savoury red. This great value Mourvèdre would work perfectly, as would other southern French reds such as Cahors, Madiran or a good Corbières.

THE COTSWOLD GIN PANTRY

Grilled mackerel with Butler's lemon and cardamom gin, sweet chilli glaze and mixed bean salad

Stopham Estate Pinot Gris, West Sussex 2013 £16

We consider this fresh beauty from Sussex to be one of the very best English still wines and it will ably handle the spice and gin aromatics. Ideally enjoy outside with great company!

GRANT HARRINGTON

Leeks cooked on an open fire, a whole roast brown trout and a sauce made from melted butter, egg yolks and the burnt outer shell of the leeks

Church Hanbrewery Oxfordshire Rauk Beer £3.70

This tiny, experimental brewery in Church Hanborough produces this Bavarian style smoke beer, which we would love to open with this fire-cooked trout, preferably close to the fire.

JACOB'S CHOPHOUSE

Roast rib of beef

Chateau de Chambert Malbec, Cahors 2010 £19

This is sophisticated man-food and needs a big classy red to go with it. The Cahors Malbec we've chosen features a generous, round palate of red berries and oaky spice, well supported by its elegant tannin structure.

JACOBS & FIELD

King prawn and coriander pizza with San Francisco sourdough

Montresor 'Campo Valentino' Lugana DOC, Lombardia 2014 £12

From the southern shores of Lake Garda, with subtle peachy stone fruit, a dash of lime and taut acidity. This wine will happily support the gambas, coriander and chilli flavours.

JACOB'S INN

Roast Cornish hake with crab and herb crust, Parmesan polenta chips, dill and saffron cream sauce

Domaine Langlois-Chateau, Saumur Blanc, Loire 2014 £11.25

This beautiful hake dish needs a wine that won't overpower the delicate flavours of the crab and hake, yet with a little acidity to stand up to the saffron cream sauce. This Loire Valley Chenin has lifted floral freshness and just enough weight. A lengthy citrus fruit finish will work beautifully with sauce.

THE WOODSTOCK ARMS
Slow roast Oxfordshire pork belly with quince and pine nut stuffing, fondant potato, buttered beans and mustard sauce
Meerlust Estate Chardonnay, Stellenbosch 2011 £20
Many would opt for a red, but a weighty white like this gorgeous Chardy is our choice. Intriguingly complex, full and generous ripe tropical fruit and creaminess balanced by a pure minerality and a long finish. Enjoy with the best of friends.

KAT ORMAN
Lemon and rosemary char-grilled spatchcock poussin, salsa verde, pearl barley, watercress, asparagus and crème fraîche
'The Oddity' Royal Tokaji dry Furmint 2013 £12
This herbal chicken dish with asparagus, mustard and gherkins needs a white with fresh acidity and spice to stand up to it. This dry Hungarian Tokaji does exactly that.

THE KITCHEN FARNBOROUGH
Roast Cotswold white chicken, herb potato dumplings, baby vegetables, saffron broth
Domaine du Petit Metris 'Clos de la Marche' Savennieres 2013 £16
A favourite of sommeliers, this dry, toasty and mineral-crisp Loire Chenin Blanc will complement the herby starchy potato dumplings and roast chicken wonderfully.

THE KITCHEN FARNBOROUGH
Garden rhubarb, strawberries and custard
Domaine de Grange Neuve, Monbazillac (500ml) 2011 £10
These classic rhubarb and custard flavours cry out for a classic pudding wine and this 'noble rot' French offering will not disappoint.

MILLER OF MANSFIELD
Wiltshire hogget lamb, confit onion, Jerusalem artichoke purée & hot pot
Cepas Viejas Bobal 2013 £11
Full-bodied old-vine dark-skinned Bobal from eastern Spain is perfect for lamb. Together this will make this dish the ultimate comfort food.

THE MUDDY DUCK
Duck and bacon salad
Ironstone Vineyards Lodi Petite Sirah 2013 £13
It's an unusual red variety from Lodi in California but we must recommend it. The damson fruit and sweet spice flavours will be spot on for this aromatic duck dish with hoisin sauce.

THE MUDDY DUCK
Fish stew
Baron de Badassiere Picpoul de Pinet 2015 £9
Clean, crisp, refreshing and fashionable; this southern French white is made for seafood. A match to imagine yourself relaxing on a sunny day near the coast.

THE MUDDY DUCK
Sticky toffee 'bockerglory'
Two Birds Salted Caramel Vodka £33
Keep this English salted caramel vodka in the freezer and serve it straight as an indulgent addition to this fun dessert. Alternatively sip a malmsey Madeira or PX sherry.

NATURAL BREAD
Bread pudding
Chambers Rosewood Vineyards 'Rutherglen Muscat', Rutherglen (375ml) £13.50
This sweet Aussie classic full of raisin, orange peel, dried fruit and rose flavours will be an indulgent delight with this sweet spice filled bread pudding.

THE NUT TREE INN
Ginger panna cotta with Yorkshire rhubarb
King's Ginger Liqueur £24
King's Ginger is a drink made for Edward VII to keep him warm while driving his horseless carriage. We suggest you try 'the king's tonic', a measure of King's Ginger with a dash of Angostura bitters, tonic water and a slice of lemon. A lovely refreshing treat with this beautiful dessert. And please keep off the road.

THE OXFORD ARMS
Smoked haddock tart
CVNE Barre- fermented Rioja Blanco 2014 £10
The oak and smoky flavours of this white Rioja will work well with the full on flavours of the smoked fish, whist not being as heavy and creamy as an oaked-aged Chardonnay.

THE OXFORD CHEESE COMPANY
Isisflette
Friedrich Wilhelm Gymnasium 'Graacher Himmelreich' Riesling Spätlese Trocken, Mosel 2012 £16

Tartiflette is very versatile when matching with wine. A hearty southern Rhône red such as Gigondas could work, but perhaps opt for something more refreshing like this dry Mosel Riesling, one of our favourite wines.

THE OXFORD KITCHEN
Lamb loin with taboulé and confit baby tomatoes
Domaine des Tourelles 2012 £11

From the old Lebanese Bekaa Valley wine region, this wine has deep cherry and savoury cedar oak flavours. We're not sure what could go better with the lamb, herb and tomato flavours.

THE OXFORD KITCHEN
Strawberry panna cotta
Innocent Bystander Yarra Valley Pink Moscato 2015 £9 or £6 for 375ml

Slightly sparkling, low alcohol (5.5%) sorbet-like Australian wine. The light, sweet red fruits in this wine will work excellently with this strawberry panna cotta.

PLANTATION CHOCOLATES
Nut praline
Ramos Pinto 'RP10' Quinta de Ervamoira Tawny Port (500ml) £19

With notes of caramel and hazelnut, this Port has the flavour and sweetness to really complement these chocolate pralines perfectly. What a treat!

PIERREPONTS CAFÉ
Baked lemon sole, with beetroot and pea risotto and a Parmesan crisp
Chateau de Belleverne 'Le Cru des Amoureux', Saint-Amour 2014 £11

Usually red wine and delicate fish should be avoided, but with this cooked in red wine, a low tannin wine such as this ripe red fruit Beau Jolais Villages from 'the Cru of the lovers' will work a treat.

THE POINTER
Veal pie
Wieninger Wiener Riesling 2015 £13.70

This Austrian dry Riesling will pair wonderfully with this veal pie cooked in white wine. Or if you prefer red, English rose veal could work wonderfully with a Pinot Noir or Loire Cabernet Franc.

THE POINTER
Blood orange posset
Causes & Cures Semi-dry White Vermouth (500ml) £18

One of our favourite finds, this Aussie vermouth is a real treat. Serve over ice with a twist of orange and a cracked bay leaf… yum.

THE QUINCE TREE
Scrumper's Scotch egg
Shotover Prospect pale ale 500ml £2.30

This British classic snack surely deserves a classic British pale ale and Shotover brewery's delightfully hoppy Prospect is one of the best. It's only from Horspath, at the bottom of Shotover hill!

THE QUINCE TREE
Mushroom tortellini
Poggio San Polo, Rosso di Montalcino 2014 £18

We had thought Pinot Noir initially, but then veered towards this Tuscan red, this beautifully balanced little brother of the great Brunello with this rich mushroom pasta dish will be spot on.

THE QUINCE TREE
Kedgeree
Alvi's Drift 'Signature' Viognier 2015 £9

Smoky, spicy kedgeree with this vibrant, slightly perfumed apricot filled fruit bomb from the Worcester region of South Africa will be quite a treat.

THE QUINCE TREE
Carpaccio of venison, Parmesan emulsion
Glen Carlou Pinot Noir, Paarl 2013 £13

This lovely, low tannin red has enough acidity and red fruit for this carpaccio with garnish and vinaigrette. It also offers an underlying rich gaminess to stand up to the venison.

THE QUINCE TREE

Macarons

Church Hanbrewery Rasp Bea £3.70

What to have with macarons and raspberry coulis? Surely a raspberry beer such as this West Oxfordshire delight…

ROSS & ROSS FOOD

Slow-roasted shoulder of English lamb, boulangère potatoes & salsa verde

Legaris Roble, Ribera del Duero DO 2014 £10

Melt in the mouth slow-roasted lamb will be wonderful with this medium-bodied, gently-oaked red, with enough fresh acidity to cut through the fat and not clash with the salsa verde.

SUDBURY HOUSE

Iberico pork chop & chorizo

Madai 'Origen' Mencia 2014 £11.50

This deceptively dark and very drinkable red wine from north west Spain is actually low in tannin, with lots of ripe fruit, and has the fresh acidity to cut through the fat beautifully.

SUDBURY HOUSE

Cherry cheesecake cannelloni

Timmermans Kriek Belgian Cherry Beer £3

Belgian cherry beer is an obvious choice for this cherry cheesecake, but if you would prefer wine go for either the delicate sorbet-like Innocent Bystander Pink Moscato (£9) or Croft Pink Port (£13) with a splash of soda water and mint.

TUTU DELICIOUS

Raspberry truffles

Mas de Lavail 'Expression', Maury, Rivesaltes, Roussillon 2012 (375ml) £11.50

This Southern French sweet red is a great alternative to Port. It's lighter with more red fruit flavours, yet enough intensity to match these lovely raspberry truffles.

UE COFFEE ROASTERS

Coffee rubbed brisket

Diemersfontein Western Cape 'Coffee Pinotage' 2013 £13

A big Douro red could work very well, but we have to recommend this South African red, which does not actually contain coffee! The winemaker uses secret methods and a well-toasted barrel to bring smoky coffee flavours to the wine.

WHITE HART FYFIELD

Roasted rump of Cotswold lamb, black olive & feta tart with ratatouille

Jean-Luc Colombo Les Collines de Laure Syrah 2014 £12

Made in the Northern Rhone, this Syrah has enough body for the lamb rump, whilst retaining fresh acidity for the ratatouille and salty feta and olives. What a treat!

THE WHITE HART FYFIELD

Chocolate marquise, lime ice cream and spiced caramel popcorn

Alvear Pedro Ximenez de Aviada 2013 £16

Here we have a very sweet, caramel coloured vintage PX from Montilla Moriles in southern Spain. Serve it chilled and see it bring out the cocoa, cinnamon and ginger in this pud.

THE WHITE HART MINSTER LOVELL

Passion fruit panna cotta/banana cake

Domaine Cazes Vin Doux Naturel 'Ambre', Rivesaltes (375ml) 1998 £16

If matching for the panna cotta and the raspberry and rose garnish, the sweet and lightly sparkling Innocent Bystander Pink Moscato (£9) would be perfect. But the banana cake calls for something a bit richer like this stunning barrel-aged 'Ambre' pudding wine.

THE WILD RABBIT

Quail

Snapper Rock Pinot Noir, Marlborough 2014 £14

The slight gaminess of the quail will work wonderfully with this gorgeous kiwi Pinot Noir. It has the brightness of red berry fruit and slightly spicy, savoury undertones that combines so well with the bird. And you'd struggle to find a Burgundy less than £40 that compares.

THE WILD RABBIT

White chocolate sphere, caramelised chocolate, Yorkshire rhubarb and strawberries

Strawberry Mojito

Cocktail time! Concoct a Strawberry Mojito by muddling lime quarters, mint leaves, strawberries and course sugar. Stir in white rum and soda water until the sugar dissolves. Getting the right balance of lime to sugar is essential. Pour over ice.

Hidden CHARMS

They say never judge a book by its cover... and when it comes to The Baskerville, there was never a truer word spoken. Behind the unassuming 1930s façade lies an award-winning pub restaurant with true quality at its heart.

You won't find the stereotypical trendy modernised country pub at The Baskerville. Walking through the door is a step back in time... a warm welcome awaits you, a reminder of the traditional, family-run village inns of the past.

Situated in Lower Shiplake on the Thames Path, The Baskerville is only a short walk to the river and Henley-on-Thames. Set in the heart of its community, the walls display the twin passions of the area – rowing and rugby – with memorabilia and signed international shirts in abundance. It retains a 'proper' bar with four cask beers, three of them from renowned local breweries.

Roaring log fires create the warm and inviting atmosphere in the winter, then, come the summer, people gather in the beautiful garden to enjoy al fresco dining and a relaxed ambience – dogs are welcome in the garden (and bar area) too.

Under the same ownership for over 12 years, the front of house is managed by the owner's son, Kevin Hannah. Customer service is almost an obsession for Kevin who, along with his friendly and knowledgeable team, goes out of his way to ensure everyone who visits is greeted like an old friend – and to be honest, many of them are! Under Kevin's watch, everybody leaves with a smile on their face having had a great dining experience.

The adherence to tradition, however, does not extend to The Baskerville's food. The menus evolve with the seasons and offer a tempting range of dishes and daily-changing specials. Great care is taken over the provenance of the produce used and head chef Jamie Herridge shares the owner's passion for ethical sourcing.

Working alongside trusted suppliers, Jamie looks for meat, poultry and game that has been compassionately farmed and locally sourced, as well as searching for delicious fresh fish from sustainable stocks. Jamie's dishes are based on classical cuisine presented in a modern European style. Cooked to order using freshly delivered ingredients, they are perfectly balanced in flavours and seasoning, winning back many repeat customers as well as attracting visitors from further afield thanks to a plethora of accolades and inclusion in many of the top food guides.

The wine list, which includes many of the owner's personal favourites, extends to sixty bins with an impressive fifteen available by the glass. There is also an extensive malt whisky collection, betraying the owner's Scottish origins.

The Baskerville
BOUILLABAISSE

This beautiful dish is a traditional Provençal fish stew and here it contains chunks of luxurious red mullet, monkfish and sea bass, as well as fresh mussels. Serves 4

Ingredients

For the bouillabaisse broth:

200ml olive oil

2 fennel bulbs, roughly chopped

2 red peppers, roughly chopped

10g sea salt

4g crushed black pepper

1kg fish bones

1kg plum tomatoes, roughly chopped

30g tomato paste

2 pinches saffron

2 lemons, juiced

40g butter

Salt and black pepper

For the rouille:

3 egg yolks

2g salt

Black pepper

1 lemon, juiced

1 pinch saffron

1 pinch cayenne pepper

200ml olive oil

200ml vegetable oil

4 garlic cloves

To plate:

2 red mullet fillets

200g monkfish, skinned

2 sea bass fillets

12 mussels, cleaned

2g basil leaves, chopped

2g parsley, chopped

Toasted baguette croutons (3 per serving)

Method

To make the bouillabaisse broth, put the olive oil into a large pan over a medium heat. Once hot, add the fennel and cook for 3-4 minutes without colouring it. Add the red peppers, sea salt and pepper and cook for another 2-3 minutes. Add the fish bones and tomatoes, then cover with water to a depth of 2½cm and bring to a simmer. Skim off any residue, add the tomato paste and saffron and bring back to a simmer. Cook for 1½ hours until reduced by approximately one-third.

Use a stick blender to mix to a smooth sauce and then pour through a fine sieve, pressing the solids with a ladle to extract all the liquid. Then pour the bouillabaisse broth through a fine chinois, this time without pressing.

Add the lemon juice then pour into a blender and add the butter. Blend and check the seasoning before passing again through a fine sieve. Chill until needed.

To make the rouille, whisk the egg yolks with the seasoning, lemon juice, saffron and cayenne pepper. Mix the olive oil and vegetable oil together and slowly add in a thin stream, whisking continuously. Stir in the garlic. Add a little warm water to thin down, if needed. Set aside until needed.

Cut the sea bass, red mullet and monkfish into 50g pieces and season lightly with salt and pepper.

Heat 500ml of the bouillabaisse to a simmer. Add the monkfish and mussels then poach for 3 minutes. Next add the sea bass and red mullet, cooking gently for another 7-8 minutes.

While the fish is cooking, spread the rouille on the toasted croutons and bake in the oven at 180°C for 3 minutes.

Once the fish is cooked, add the basil and the parsley and serve immediately.

Free-range FLAVOUR

The beautiful Oxfordshire countryside is the idyllic setting for Blue Tin Produce, a small family-run farm in Ipsden, where rare-breed meat is reared using traditional and natural methods and sold from the on-site farm shop.

'How meat used to taste' is the description that they hear most often from their customers at Blue Tin Produce. Succulent, tasty and tender, the free-range meat from this beautiful little family farm is a world away from supermarket cuts. Although it's safe to say there have been a few challenges along the way for Emma and Jed, who began their journey in 2002.

They started their business with ten Gloucester Old Spot pigs, a rare breed that is perfectly suited to being bred slowly outdoors. From the day these pigs are born they are free to roam in the large paddocks complete with wallows and houses filled with clean straw.

During the early days Jed and Emma put in a huge amount of hard work – they remember endlessly fixing broken fences, chasing escaped piglets and defrosting frozen hose pipes in winter. However they received advance orders for all ten original pigs and the customers were wowed by the incredible flavour of the pork. The slow rearing and outdoor lifestyle gives the pigs a layer of fat that adds remarkable depth of flavour and extraordinary succulence.

Today, rare-breed Dexter beef has been added to their stock, with a herd of 86 cattle built up over the last five years. Not only do the cattle enjoy the same free-range lifestyle as the Gloucester Old Spot pigs, the meat is hung for 28 days to ensure the very best flavour is achieved. It is proving so popular among local restaurants, pubs and their farm shop customers that they have been nominated for and are finalists in the coveted Countryside Alliance Awards for local produce!

Why not pop in to their farm shop to try it for yourself? Their sausages are hugely popular (with a range of flavours from the best-selling originals to pork and Stilton, honey roast and a hot, hot, hot pork and chilli), as are the bacon, gammon, Dexter beef burgers and free-range eggs. You can also buy Black Welsh Mountain lamb and mutton reared by Jed's uncle on the neighbouring farm, free-range locally reared bronze turkeys and geese at Christmas time and a plethora of other local products from chutneys, vegetables and cheese to fresh bread, cakes and honey.

What doesn't come from their own farm tends to be sourced from within five miles of Blue Tin Produce – a celebration of the creative talents of their neighbours all brought together under one roof.

PROVENANCE
INFORMATION

Apple Juice
0 miles

Jams, Jellies, Pickles,
Chilli stuff &
Chutneys. 5-10 miles

Bread
2 miles

Logs
4 miles

Free Range
Eggs
0 miles

Veg
0 miles
English

Free Range
Pork
0 miles

Lamb & Mutton
2 miles

Dexter Beef
0 miles

EGGS

Blue Tin Produce

Blue Tin Produce
20% off all our frozen meats this month!

The quintessential VILLAGE SHOP

Chadlington is a village that stands out as a lovely place to visit for many reasons – its vibrant community spirit, its well-used little high street and, above all, its famous village shop.

In 2001, when the village shop was set to close down, the determined people of Chadlington (which is just south of Chipping Norton) got together to keep the store running. Since then, the shop has formed an important part of life in Chadlington, providing top-quality food and a warm welcome to boot. It's renowned as a place where people from all over Oxfordshire come to sample the gastronomic delights on offer.

What makes Chadlington Quality Foods so special is its true 'village store' feel. The shelves are lined with store-cupboard essentials, many made by local producers and independent businesses, meaning that Chadlington residents can always pop in to buy basics, from oils, tinned tomatoes, flour, spices and pasta to fruits and vegetables, eggs, milk and fresh bread.

The cheese counter offers an outstanding array of fine cheeses, which are selected from some of Oxfordshire and Britain's finest producers, as well as those classics from our neighbours in Europe. The deli counter contains a tempting collection of meats, too, with British charcuterie holding its own against the mighty French, Spanish and Italian options.

Local people who grow their own produce supply some of the fresh fruits and vegetables for sale in the shop – Chadlington Quality Foods is always keen to sell local produce where possible to reduce their environmental impact and support the local economy. Plus, being lucky enough to be surrounded by such a wealth of delicious natural bounty, the team at the shop consider it a priority to make the most of everything Oxfordshire has to offer.

The talented team are busy in the on-site kitchen every day making delicious snacks for the deli counter – quiches, dips, cakes and pastries, for example, as well as luxurious jams and chutneys with seasonal fruits and vegetables.

Many a local party has benefited from the skills within the Chadlington Quality Foods kitchen – their catering service is ideal for gatherings or events. Pop along and have a chat to the team and they'll do their best to put together a catering package to suit your needs.

According to The Daily Telegraph, Chadlington is "everything a village should be" – and the lovely village shop is a huge part of that. Not only a vital part of everyday life for the locals, but a reason for people from the surrounding areas to come and visit the village, stock up on fine foods and enjoy a taste of Oxfordshire village life.

Cherry Vine tomatoes £7.00 kg.

CHADLINGTON QUALITY FOODS
CQF

Chadlington Quality Foods
APRICOT AND ALMOND TART

Homemade sweet shortcrust pastry filled with a mouth-watering apricot and almond filling – this recipe never fails to please. Serves 8

Ingredients

For the pastry:

125g butter

100g icing sugar

Pinch of salt

250g plain flour

2 egg yolks

2 tbsp cold milk or water

For the filling:

260g ground almonds

130g icing sugar

65g caster sugar

3 eggs

1 tsp almond essence

400g tin apricots, drained

25g flaked almonds

Method

You will need a 23cm loose-bottom flan tin.

For the pastry

Cream together the butter, sugar and salt and then rub in the flour and egg yolks. Once the mixture has come together to look like coarse breadcrumbs, add the milk/water. Pat and gently work together to form a ball of dough – do not overwork the pastry. Wrap the ball of pastry in cling film and chill in the fridge for at least 1 hour.

For the filling

Put all the ingredients, with the exception of the apricots and flaked almonds, into a large bowl and mix together.

Preheat the oven to 160°C/Gas 3.

To assemble the tart

Grease a 23cm flan tin. Roll out the pastry on a well-floured surface and use it to line the greased tin. Trim off any excess pastry but allow a little overhang for shrinkage. Prick the base all over. Line the tin with baking paper and baking beans, and bake blind in the preheated oven for 12-15 minutes.

Remove the paper and beans and bake for a further 5 minutes to dry out the pastry. Remove the pastry case from the oven and increase the oven temperature to 180°C.

Carefully pour the filling mixture into the baked pastry case. Decorate with apricot pieces and sprinkle with flaked almonds.

Bake in the centre of the preheated oven for 15 minutes and then drop heat to 175°C for a further 30 minutes until risen, golden and firm to the touch. Leave to cool in the tin until firm.

Chadlington Quality Foods
SALMON AND BROCCOLI PIE

Warming and comforting, this is delicious home-cooking at its best, and a perfect way to make the most of seasonal local vegetables. Serves 6

Ingredients

1.5kg potatoes, peeled and cut into chunks

70g butter

1 large head of broccoli, cut into bite-sized pieces.

3 medium leeks, chopped

1 bunch spring onions, chopped

900g fresh salmon

2 tbsp fresh dill, chopped

2 tbsp parsley, chopped

25g plain flour

400ml milk

200ml double cream

4 tbsp wholemeal breadcrumbs

2 tbsp Parmesan cheese, grated

Salt and pepper

Method

Cook the potatoes in a pan of boiling water, then drain. Mash with 25g of the butter and season.

Cook the broccoli and drain well.

Sauté the leeks in 20g of the butter, until cooked but not coloured. Remove from the heat and stir in the chopped spring onion.

Preheat the oven to 180°C/Gas 4.

Bake the salmon in the preheated oven for 15 minutes or until just cooked. Leave the oven on. Flake the salmon into good-size chunks and sprinkle over the base of an ovenproof serving dish.

Scatter the cooked broccoli and the leek and spring onion mixture over the salmon. Season and add the chopped herbs.

To make the sauce

Melt the remaining 25g butter in a pan, add the flour and stir for 1-2 minutes over a medium heat. Take the pan off the heat and whisk in the milk and cream. Return to the heat and simmer for 8-10 minutes, stirring continuously. Season with salt and pepper.

Pour the sauce over the salmon and vegetable mixture. Top with mashed potatoes and finish with the breadcrumbs and Parmesan. Bake in the preheated oven for 30-40 minutes until golden brown.

Top of the
CHERRY TREE

Having left the bright lights of London in 2004, Douglas Green relocated to historic Henley-on-Thames to realise his dream of starting up his own independent pub company. Beginning with flagship pub The Little Angel, the charming Cherry Tree Inn followed in 2012.

Douglas, from a background of working with high profile chefs, owning hotels and subsequently a ground breaking gastro pub company in the late '90s, wanted to create great pubs with fantastic food that were welcoming to all just outside London. When an opportunity presented itself to take on the stunning 17th century Cherry Tree Inn, Douglas leapt at the chance to extend his business to the Chiltern Hills, a designated area of Outstanding Natural Beauty.

A busy local with drinkers and foodies, don't be surprised if you see a celebrity or two; from film producers, F1 team owners and rock stars to the local farrier! The area, with its history, events and scenic countryside is also a draw for walkers, cyclists, horse riders and festival goers alike. These varied visitors to the area all frequent The Cherry Tree and can be found sitting comfortably alongside each other enjoying cracking ales, wines and Champagne as well as great food. With four luxury king-sized rooms in the barn conversion adjacent to the pub, a restful night's sleep is also assured here.

Head chef Chris Shepherd and sous chef George Pinch were recruited together from Bristol because of their consistency and enthusiasm to innovate and deliver fantastic local produce. Their ethos is about creating exciting dishes using produce that is as fresh as can be; Chris and George can often be seen wading into the woods to forage for ingredients and where they aren't able to acquire things for themselves many of the pub's suppliers are based in the local area. The front of house staff are bright, fresh, knowledgeable and friendly; this cocktail of passionate people and a beautiful location makes The Cherry Tree Inn so appealing.

With a big year round social calendar, you'll find no prettier pub with its wisteria covered exterior and welcoming spaces – expect barbecues, hog roasts, dog shows and the usual family fun associated with community pubs. The Cherry Tree and its sister The Little Angel are very much entrenched in the area, and from the number of returning regulars it's clear people really trust what they do.

The Cherry Tree Inn

WOODLAND MUSHROOM, WHITE TRUFFLE AND WILD GARLIC FLATBREADS AND POTTED RABBIT RILLETTES

Serves 4 to share

Ingredients

For the rabbit rillettes:

2 stems celery

1 red onion

2 carrots

3 cloves garlic

1 whole rabbit, oven ready

500ml Chianti red wine

4 tbsp tomato purée

2 bouquet garni

3 sprigs rosemary

Salt and pepper, to season

For the flatbreads:

500g plain flour

Pinch salt

300ml warm water

7g dried instant yeast

1 tbsp olive oil

For the topping:

200g wild mushrooms

10g white truffle

50g wild garlic

2 tbsp olive oil

50g butter

¼ tsp ground nutmeg

Method

For the rabbit rillettes

This is best done the night before or in the morning.

In a large saucepan, soften the celery, red onion, carrots and garlic on a medium heat for 3-4 minutes.

Place the rabbit into the pan, add the wine, tomato purée, rosemary and bouquet garni. Top the pan up with water, enough so the rabbit is completely submerged. Bring to a simmer, cover with the lid and turn onto a very low heat for 2½ hours; stirring gently every 30 minutes. Once cooked, allow to cool for several hours.

Once cool, remove the rabbit from the cooking stock. Using your hands, shred the meat off the carcass, be careful around the saddle as there are many small and delicate bones. Strain the stock.

Transfer the meat to a food processor. On the pulse setting, gradually add some of the strained cooking stock until a pâté texture is achieved. Then season with salt and pepper and add to a mason kilner jar. Serve chilled.

For the flatbreads

Sieve the plain flour into a mixing bowl and add a pinch of salt.

Separately, measure out 300ml of warm water, add the yeast, stir and then leave to ferment for 10 minutes.

Then add the water mixture to the flour with the oil. Combine the mixture until a dough forms. Cover the bowl with a damp cloth and leave to rise (prove) in a warm place for 1 hour.

Then, knock back the dough, kneading for several minutes until it's a good elastic consistency. Cut into 8 equal pieces and with a rolling pin, roll about 25mm thick and then cut to desired size.

Preferably, heat a skillet on a high heat, if you don't have a skillet you can use a heavy based bottom pan. Once hot, place the flatbread into the un-oiled pan for about 45 seconds to 1 minute on each side. Remove from the pan.

For the woodland mushroom, white truffle and wild garlic topping

Ensure the mushrooms are clean and clear of any grit or dirt, but are dry. Sauté the mushrooms and wild garlic in a frying pan using butter and oil. Add the nutmeg. Cook for about 4-6 minutes until golden. Top the flatbreads with the mushroom and garlic mix. Then thoroughly clean the white truffle, again to remove any dirt or grit and using a potato peeler, shave the truffle to garnish.

Serve the breads, rillettes and mushrooms immediately whilst still warm.

Christine Wallace
ST CLEMENTS DREAMY LAYER CAKE

A lavish and beautiful cake from The BBC's Great British Bake Off 2013 quarter finalist Christine Wallace. Christine lives in Oxfordshire with her family and loves to bake this beautiful cake. It can be served as a cake or as a dessert and will really impress your friends and family.
This cake will keep in the fridge for 2-3 days. Serves 8-10

Ingredients

For the cake:

4 large eggs, separated

130g caster sugar

1 lemon, grated zest only

130g self-raising flour

45g unsalted butter, melted

For the flower top:

1 packet lemon jelly

250g mandarin oranges

1 large stick of angelica

A few black grapes, halved

For the lemon syrup:

80g caster sugar

4 tbsp water

2 lemons, juiced

For the lemon mousse:

4 leaves of gelatine

4 large eggs, separated

125g caster sugar

2 small lemons, grated zest only

2 lemons, juiced

300ml double cream

A little water

To finish:

300ml double cream

Method

Preheat the oven to 200°C/180°C fan and grease and line a 23cm solid-bottom cake tin.

For the cake, place the eggs, sugar and lemon zest in the bowl of a stand mixer and beat on fast speed until it has doubled in bulk and is very pale in colour.

Sieve the flour and carefully fold into the egg mixture, being careful not to lose the precious air you have put in!

Gently pour the melted butter around the edge and fold that in, ensuring that there is no residue of butter left in the bottom of the bowl.

Spoon into the prepared tin and bake for approximately 25 minutes or until golden and a skewer comes out clean when inserted into the centre of the cake. Leave in the tin for a few minutes and then turn out on to a wire rack to cool. Wash the tin in very hot water to remove all grease, and dry thoroughly.

Make the jelly as directed to just under 1 pint. Pour between one-third and one-half of the jelly into the cake tin and carefully place into the fridge to set. Leave the rest of the jelly to one side, but not in the fridge.

Thoroughly drain the mandarin oranges and make sure they are not too 'wet'. Open out the angelica and flatten with a knife. Cut out a long thin stem for your main flower plus two shorter ones for the 'shoots'.

When the jelly is set in the tin, remove it from the fridge. Create a large flower in the centre of the jelly using the long stem, black grapes as the flower centre and spreading out the mandarins as petals. Using the shorter stems, form two smaller flowers as off shoots of the main ones. Place back in the fridge.

Now place the remaining jelly into the fridge and watch it carefully. When just beginning to thicken, carefully spoon over the flowers in the tin, making sure all is covered by jelly and being careful not to displace the fruit. Replace in the fridge.

Make the lemon syrup by placing all the ingredients in a small pan. Bring to the boil and simmer until the sugar has completely dissolved for about 5 minutes. Cool.

Make the lemon mousse. Soak the gelatine leaves in a little water until soft. Beat the egg yolks, caster sugar and lemon zest until thick and creamy. Place the soft gelatine into a small pan and add a little of the lemon juice to cover. Slowly heat stirring until just clear from the heat. Cool slightly then add the remaining lemon juice. Add the juice and gelatine to the egg mix and combine.

Beat the cream until a soft peak consistency (do not let the cream go really stiff). Fold into the lemon mix then beat the egg whites until stiff and gently fold in until all combined. Leave for about 10 minutes.

To make up the gateau, cut the cake in half horizontally. Line the tin above the jelly with some lightly buttered baking parchment. Place half the mousse on top of your flowers and jelly in the tin. Liberally dab the cut side of one of the sponges with half the lemon syrup using a pastry brush. Place lemon-side up gently on top of the mousse and, using the back of a spoon, slightly flatten the edge of the sponge hard against the side of the tin.

Repeat this process using the rest of the mousse and the remaining half of sponge but this time place the lemon syrup on the cut side and place that side down on to the mousse.

Cover loosely with cling film and place in the fridge for at least 4 hours or preferably make the day before you want to use it.

When ready to serve, dip the bottom of the tin into very hot water for literally a couple of seconds, too much and you will melt your jelly! Place a plate on top of the tin and invert, then remove the tin and peel off the parchment. To finish whip up the double cream to piping consistency and pipe large shells around the edge of your cake.

The Cogges Kitchen
KELMSCOTT BACON & CHEDDAR MUFFINS

The Cogges Kitchen makes the best of its stunning surrounds in the old milking parlour at Cogges Manor Farm by serving up hearty dishes inspired by the nearby walled garden and orchard. Sarah and Rob, who also own artisan café Coffeesmith in Witney, pride themselves on their daily-changing menu that makes the most of locally sourced seasonal produce. From breakfast to brunch, hot lunches, salads, sandwiches, afternoon tea, cakes and ice cream, there's plenty to choose from down at the farm. Serves 12

Ingredients

1 tsp oil

150g bacon, diced into small pieces

250g wholemeal self-raising flour

2 tsp baking powder

½ tsp bicarbonate of soda

¼ tsp salt

2 eggs

80g unsalted butter, melted and cooled

200ml natural yoghurt

Finely chopped fresh herbs, parsley or chives to taste

150g mature cheddar, grated

Method

Heat the oven to 200°C and line a deep muffin tin with 12 paper 'tulip' style cases.

Warm the oil over a medium heat and fry the bacon until just crisp. Lift the bacon from the pan with a slotted spoon and drain on kitchen paper.

In a large bowl, whisk together the flour, baking powder, bicarbonate of soda and salt. In a jug, whisk the eggs, butter and yoghurt, stir them into the flour mixture with a spatula until just combined, then fold in the cooled bacon, herbs and two-thirds of the cheese until just evenly distributed. (Do not overwork the mixture).

Using an ice-cream scoop to ensure uniform filling, scoop the mixture into the muffin tin as quickly as possible, sprinkle on the rest of the cheese, and bake for about 20 minutes, until the tops are golden and a skewer inserted into the centre of a muffin comes out clean.

Leave to cool before serving.

Desserts DELIVERED

There is a simple ethos behind the wonderful Cotswold Baking, where cakes, desserts and all manner of sweet treats are made fresh to order – to bring the finest quality bakes to the Cotswolds.

When it comes to baking, the incredibly talented Paul Barlow-Heal certainly knows his dough from his doughnuts. The man behind the success of Cotswold Baking has been passionate about pastry since the age of 14, when he began his first job working part-time in a bakery. Since then, he has worked as an apprentice under Michel Roux Snr at The Waterside Inn in Bray, learning everything he could from the famous chef, before moving to Oxfordshire and taking over a landmark Cotswolds pub with his wife.

After 8 happy years at the pub, Paul decided it was time for a change and he was drawn back to his roots and his love of baking. Now armed with years of experience, knowledge and expertise, he set about creating Cotswold Baking with the aim of bringing quality cakes and desserts direct to people's doors.

His busy kitchen is a hive of activity throughout the week as he creates popular products for stalls at Deddington, Charlbury and Adderbury farmers markets, as well as working on projects for private clients. At the markets, people stop by for a chat and request things for him to make to order. There is no set menu to limit your choice – with such a wealth of expertise at his fingertips, Paul can create anything you like and he doesn't shy away from a challenge!

From simple cakes for an afternoon tea to a towering croquembouche or a tiered wedding cake, Paul loves discussing the flavours, ingredients and decoration ideas with his clients. Every cake or dessert is personal and each one is developed and baked to order. He is well-known for creating gluten-free options for people and will happily develop recipes to make gluten-free cakes that deliver on taste and texture.

For Paul, quality is key. Starting with the finest ingredients is the best way to ensure incredible results, which is why he always uses British butter, free-range eggs and local flour. He even uses walnuts and hazelnuts which are grown on the farm where his kitchen is based. With the Cotswolds offering such bountiful produce right on his doorstep – as well as superb local suppliers and the finest fresh produce – sourcing the very best ingredients is a piece of cake.

Cotswold Baking
RHUBARB & ALMOND STREUSEL TART

This gluten-free recipe from Cotswold Baking is perfect when British rhubarb is in season. Serve warm with crème fraîche or vanilla ice cream. Serves 8

Ingredients

100g rhubarb jam or apricot jam

500g rhubarb cut into 2cm squares, lightly poached and drained

60g flaked almonds

For the pastry:

500g gluten-free plain flour, plus extra for dusting

180g icing sugar

Pinch of salt

200g unsalted butter (cold)

2 whole eggs (100g), beaten

75ml cold water

For the frangipane:

200g unsalted butter

200g caster sugar

200g whole eggs

200g ground almonds

30g gluten-free plain flour

Pinch of gluten-free baking powder

For the streusel:

65g gluten-free plain flour

40g unsalted butter

70g light soft brown sugar

½ tsp ground cinnamon

Method

For the pastry

In a food processor blend all the dry ingredients together with the butter until a breadcrumb texture forms, then tip into a large bowl and add the beaten egg and water and bring the dough together, (it will seem very wet, but will firm up in the fridge). Wrap in cling film and refrigerate for 30 minutes.

For the frangipane

Beat together the butter and sugar until pale, then gradually add the eggs, one at a time. Finally mix in the ground almonds, flour and baking powder. Set aside.

For the streusel

Put all the ingredients into a mixing bowl and mix until they come together and start binding. Set aside.

Preheat the oven to 150°C. Using gluten-free flour for dusting, roll out half of your pastry (rewrap and freeze the remaining pastry for next time) and line a 10-inch loose bottom tart case. Line your pastry case with 2 layers of cling film making sure to overlap the edges, then add baking beans or uncooked rice and bake the case for 30 minutes to part-bake the tart case. Remove from oven and leave to cool.

Increase the oven temperature to 180°C. Remove the baking beans and cling film, spread the jam over the base of the tart case, then add the frangipane, spreading an even layer. Scatter over the cooked drained rhubarb, finishing with the flaked almonds and finally scatter pieces of the streusel topping over the top.

Bake in the preheated oven for 20-25 minutes until golden brown, then leave to cool slightly in the tart case.

Gin O'CLOCK

Enclosed within a 16th century stone country house in the rural Cotswold village of Clanfield is a gin lover's paradise...

The seed of an idea was planted many moons ago by Martin Agius, founder of various restaurants, brasseries and a hotel, over the last 35 years, in Oxfordshire. The driving force behind this booming, boozy business, he brings his fountain of knowledge and skill to make the perfect G&T for many. Locally known as "The Gin Man" he has created a team of gin connoisseurs.

Originally a small but considered gin shelf at The Cotswold Plough Hotel it was the talking point for discerning customers that were intrigued as to what went in their G&T.

Due to its popularity and the gin connoisseurs' abundance of enthusiasm, the shelf quickly overflowed. Today it consists of a dedicated room, cascading with bottles of gin and genièvre from all over the world. Guests are invited to explore the shelves by opening and smelling numerous bottles to aid their selection and members of the team are on hand for recommendations if needed.

Since evolving into The Cotswold Gin Pantry of today, it attracts people from far and wide to sample the extensive collection and partake in an exciting range of gin experiences such as gin tastings, Gin blending and bespoke opportunities to blend your own bottle of gin. It is so much more than just a gin bar, with popular events running throughout the week including Fever-Tree Fridays, Gin Lazy Sundays and Bank Holiday gin specials – all sessions can also be bought as gift vouchers from www.ginpantry.co.uk.

The Cotswold Gin Pantry would not be complete without gin's partners in crime; complementing the collection you'll find a huge variety of tonics, mixers, bitters and garnishes on offer. The connoisseurs believe it's all about experimenting with botanicals, participants having fun, taking creative risk and inventing something exciting and delicious.

Always looking to expand, customers are challenged to call before arrival to check whether a specific gin is in stock. If not and it passes muster with the gin connoisseurs, then you're invited for one free three course meal within the hotel in exchange for bringing the bottle with you.

The Cotswold Gin Pantry housed within The Cotswold Plough provides a wealth of inspiration to the culinary concepts behind the scenes within the kitchen. On the menus you will find dishes that push the imaginative boundaries of taste, with botanical influence, such as grilled mackerel with Butler's lemon and cardamom gin, sweet chilli glaze mixed bean salad; alongside British classics like braised beef cheeks with sweet potato gratin, purple sprouting and buttered kale or their famous beer battered fish and chips.

A versatile space, in a stunning location with a spectacular frontage, The Cotswold Plough is able to accommodate weddings, business lunches, gin team building events, private dining and more. It has a relaxed country dining ambiance, 11 beautifully decorated, comfortable rooms for those wishing to stay and with the passionate and expert staff it makes this gin palace a true gem of the Oxfordshire culinary scene.

The Cotswolds Gin Pantry
GRILLED MACKEREL WITH BUTLER'S LEMON AND CARDAMOM GIN, SWEET CHILLI GLAZE AND MIXED BEAN SALAD

Serves 6

Ingredients

6 large boneless mackerel fillets

A selection of mangetout, green beans, broad beans, sugar snaps

Lemon juice

Sea salt

Extra virgin olive oil

For the glaze:

1 tsp chilli flakes

½ cup light brown sugar

2 tsp soy sauce

4 tsp lemon juice

¼ tsp allspice

To serve:

Butler's lemon and cardamom gin, for drizzling

Method

Prepare the beans by blanching in separate batches until cooked, but have a crunch. Refresh under cold water, dress with lemon, sea salt and oil.

Put all the glaze ingredients in a small pan. Bring to the boil. Cook until it starts to thicken, remove from heat.

Place the fish on an oiled tray lined with foil. Grill for 2 minutes, turn and grill for one minute. Aim for it to be pink in the middle.

Brush with the glaze and return to the grill. Grill until the glaze starts to burn. Serve on the beans, with a drizzle of Butler's lemon and cardamom gin.

Top of THE BILLET

Despite being the first place in the UK to be dubbed a gastro pub by the media back in 1989, it's pretty hard to pigeon hole The Crooked Billet when it comes to their unique style of food.

Chef and proprietor Paul Clerehugh is nothing if not passionate about what he does. Buying the 17th century inn back in the late '80s was a huge undertaking, especially from someone with more experience on stage armed with a guitar than in a kitchen with a set of knives. Despite being entirely self-taught, Paul soon proved he is up there with the best of them as he was the first pub chef to receive the British Craft Guild of Chef's Award; previous recipients include Albert and Michel Roux, Pierre Koffmann and Raymond Blanc.

It's never been about sticking to traditions at The Crooked Billet, and more about getting the absolute most out of local produce. They cultivate much of the fruit, vegetables and salad in polytunnels and have built up connections with local growers, foragers and producers. From a friend who has a spaniel that can source truffles to mozzarella from none other than racing driver Jody Scheckter – all manner of ingredients are brought in and exchanged for a meal on the house.

The menu changes a bit every day, depending upon what's available. Dishes may range from English John Dory put simply with new season asparagus and nettle pesto to shepherd's pie with goat and wild spring garlic mash. Their rustic plates are more likely to look more on the messy side than precise and symmetrical, which is down to Paul's personal preference for the quirky that he describes as combining "big flavour with a bit of a rough edge."

To share his passion about cooking (and to satisfy the inner show off from his bygone musician days) Paul decided to host cookery demonstrations, 50 of which he did back to back last summer. Showcasing uncomplicated dishes that let the ingredients do most of the singing, these light hearted affairs have become legendary and hugely popular since their inception.

From the secret walled garden that can only be found through a maze of hedges to the mish mash of furniture among the cosy nooks and crannies inside, there's a bit of magic in the walls of The Crooked Billet – magic that's attracted many famous faces over the years. Reputable chefs like Marco Pierre White, Heston Blumenthal, James Martin and Jamie Oliver are all former diners whilst Tom Jones, Kylie Minogue, Kenneth Branagh, Matt Damon and Orlando Bloom can be caught mingling with the locals.

So how would you describe The Crooked Billet? Paul muses: "Someone put it brilliantly to me recently. They said 'imagine it in terms of music, at one end there's Elton John and at the other end you've got Ian Dury and the Blockheads. You're more the latter' which I think is spot on."

The Crooked Billet

RACK OF GOAT, SHEPHERD'S PIE

Serves 2

Ingredients

2 x 300g 3 boned, best end goat racks, well-trimmed

2 sprigs rosemary

2 cloves garlic, peeled and crushed

50g wild garlic

20g butter

200g buttery mashed potato, warm

½ tsp cumin seeds

½ tsp coriander seeds

40g goat dripping or 2 tbsp cooking oil

250g coarse minced goat shoulder

1 English onion, diced

2 sticks celery, 1cm dice

½ tsp chopped fresh thyme

2 cloves garlic, finely chopped

1 tsp tomato purée

150ml red wine

150ml goat stock

Sea salt, freshly ground pepper

Method

For the pie

Rub two goat racks with two sprigs rosemary and two crushed garlic cloves. Place the racks, rosemary and garlic in a bowl, cover with cling film and leave overnight in the fridge.

Make the topping for the shepherd's pie. Blanch the wild garlic for ten seconds in simmering water, refresh and pat dry on kitchen paper. Place in a food processor with the butter and blitz to a smooth paste.

Place mashed potato in a mixing bowl, add the wild garlic paste and mix thoroughly.

Toast the cumin and coriander seeds in a dry frying pan, no oil, for three minutes, transfer to a pestle and mortar and grind until smooth.

Place a large heavy based saucepan on the hob on a moderate heat. Add 20g (half) the goat dripping and mince, seal the meat and colour it. Add the onion, celery and thyme and cook for five or six minutes until the vegetables begin to soften.

Add the tomato purée and stir through evenly. Add the wine, then after two minutes add the stock.

For a good rich shepherd's pie filling, allow the mince to slowly cook on a soft simmer for an hour. Taste and season.

Divide the mixture between two small pie dishes, large ramekins or copper pans, top with wild garlic mash – rough up the mash surface for a crispy finish. Heat the pies in a preheated 180°C oven until the mash topping is crispy and the filling is hot.

For the racks

Remove from the marinade bowl. Discard the rosemary and garlic.

Place a suitably sized heavy-based oven proof frying pan over a moderate heat. Add the remaining 20g goat dripping.

Season the racks well with sea salt and freshly ground black pepper. Place racks fat side down in the pan, seal and colour for five minutes. Place pan in a preheated 180°C oven for 10-15 minutes then remove from the oven. Remove the racks from the pan and rest on a warm plate for 10 minutes.

In the photograph the rack of goat shepherd's pie is accompanied with cumin and honey roast heritage carrots, wilted kale, carrot purée and a sticky reduced red wine goat gravy.

The Crooked Billet

BUILDERS TEA BRULEE, MILK CHOCOLATE HOB NOBS

Makes 16 biscuits and 6 tea cups

Ingredients

For the biscuits:

50g self-raising flour

50g caster sugar

50g porridge oats

⅓ tsp bicarbonate of soda

⅓ tsp ground cinnamon

50g unsalted butter

1 tsp golden syrup

75g milk chocolate, broken into small pieces

For the builders teacups:

568ml double cream

350ml whole milk

10 tea bags

8 tbsp caster sugar

6 egg yolks

Method

Preheat the oven to 170°C.

Mix together the flour, sugar, oats, bicarbonate of soda and cinnamon. Melt the butter and syrup together with half a teaspoon of hot water in a pan. Pour this over the dry mixture and stir until well combined. Measure a teaspoon of the mixture onto a lined baking sheet and flatten each into a circle with a bottom of a cup. Repeat until you have used all of your mixture. Tidy the sides then bake for 8-9 minutes, until golden. Allow to cool. Melt the milk chocolate and brush over the top of each biscuit, alternatively you can ice the biscuits as we have in the picture.

For the teacups, preheat the oven to 170°C.

Stand six 150ml teacups in a roasting tin. Put the cream, milk and tea bags in a heavy based pan with 4 tablespoons of sugar and place on a low heat for 10 minutes. While the cream warms, whisk the egg yolks with 4 tablespoons of sugar for 5 minutes, until the yolks turn to creamy white. Bring the cream to just under boiling point and strain immediately over the yolks. Stir to combine thoroughly. Sieve the mixture into a large measuring jug. Skim off the foamy bubbles and pour through a fine tea strainer into each tea cup, filling each one two thirds full. Skim off any more bubbles.

Transfer the tin to the oven shelf. Pull the shelf out and half fill the tin with boiling water before sliding it back into place. Bake for 40 minutes. Remove from the oven, they should be firm but with a slight wobble in the middle. Allow to stand in the roasting tin with the water for a further 5 minutes. Sprinkle sugar on top of the custard and caramelise with a blow torch, or under a very hot grill until golden brown, be careful not to burn the sugar.

Remove the cups from the tin and serve immediately or leave to cool. Serve each cup on a saucer with a chocolate biscuit or two for dipping.

A deli with a DIFFERENCE

For a cup of top-quality coffee and a freshly prepared bite to eat surrounded by the most irresistible range of goodies from Oxfordshire's finest independent producers – Delicacy in Chipping Norton is nothing short of a foodie paradise.

Jon and Liz took over the Delicacy in 2014, having been won over immediately by its atmosphere and charm. They knew the area and premises well, both being locals, and simply fell in love with the character and feel of the shop.

They have kept the deli at the heart of the business, as it is such an important and well-used part of the community. The well-stocked shelves are arranged beautifully with a whole host of produce enticingly displayed – a nod to Liz's artistic background as well as her keen commitment to supporting local makers.

However, the new owners have added more, introducing a beautiful café, serving the very best artisan coffee from local company Ue Coffee. With Jon hailing from a coffee background it's no surprise that he has opted to put the finest coffee at the heart of the business. Light lunches, sandwiches, pastries and cakes accompany the wood-roasted coffee and fine teas, which can be enjoyed in the pleasant ambience of the shop or at one of the outside tables when the sun is shining.

Jon and Liz have married the deli and café seamlessly with the food that is served acting as a showcase for the ingredients they stock. If you tuck into one of chef Penny's delicious pies or savoury tarts, for example, it will have been made fresh on the premises with the charcuterie and cheese from the deli counter and the locally milled flour that adorns the shelves in the dough. The menu, like the stock, changes to reflect the seasons and availability of ingredients.

Delicacy also offers a range of catering services, as well as irresistible hampers – pop in for a chat to see what delicious local produce they can put together for you.

Delicacy
MAFTOUL ROSE SALAD

Maftoul is a traditional Palestinian grain made from organic bulgar and whole-wheat flour. The combination of ingredients we use in this salad balances all of the flavours, but quantities can be adapted to taste. This dish works well as a salad dish or served with lamb shank. You don't have to search far and wide, all of the ingredients are available from our shop. Serves 4

Ingredients

250g maftoul

Drizzle of extra virgin olive oil

2 tsp pomegranate molasses

3–4 tsp ras-el-hanout

100g black olives, stones removed, diced

½ preserved lemon, flesh removed, diced

Sprinkling of dried rose petals

2–3 tbsp pomegranate seeds

Handful of mint, roughly chopped

4–5 dried apricots, diced small

Method

Cook the maftoul in 600ml water for 20 minutes, until all of the water is absorbed. Alternatively, the maftoul can be steamed for the same amount of time.

Gently add the olive oil and pomegranate molasses to coat the maftoul.

Add the ras-el-hanout and mix well.

Add the remaining ingredients, adding extra rose petals and mint to decorate.

Alternatively, giant couscous, bulgar wheat and fregula all work well with this recipe.

Party-perfect BITES

Innovative, professional and bespoke – Fingers & Forks has been catering for Oxfordshire's events for over five years, from intimate dinner parties to extravagant wedding receptions.

Highly renowned chef Kevin Cadman is the experienced face behind the specialist catering company Fingers & Forks. He has over 20 years of first-class catering experience, having cooked in some of France's most celebrated restaurants and travelled the world cooking for private, celebrity and corporate clients.

Having settled in beautiful Oxfordshire more than 10 years ago, Kevin was won over by the region's picturesque countryside, its charming towns and its passion for quality when it comes to food. Surrounded by some of the country's most wonderful producers, Kevin set up his catering company with the aim of providing bespoke dining options and affordable luxury for Oxfordshire's residents, putting the finest quality local ingredients at the heart of every menu.

Chilterns lamb, Cotswold dairy, artisan cheeses – Fingers & Forks pride themselves on their ethical values and commitment to using sustainable seasonal produce with minimal impact to the environment and community in which we all live. And of course by using such reputable local producers, Kevin can ensure the very finest flavour too.

When it comes to what Fingers & Forks can offer, there really is no set menu. It's a truly bespoke service where the individual takes centre stage and the talented team work up a suitable menu around their budget and desires. Whether it's the perfect bite-size canapés for a small gathering, a dinner party in your own home, a wedding reception for hundreds of people or a formal corporate event, there is no occasion too big or too small.

Having worked in India, Thailand, Sri Lanka, Africa, the Middle East and across Europe, Kevin is perfectly suited to developing authentic world dishes or creating fusion flavours to suit your taste. Or perhaps a quintessentially English affair is required, where Kevin can wow guests with classic luxury or modern elegance.

For the Fingers & Forks team, the most rewarding part of what they do is working with clients in the run up to the day to ensure everything goes exactly as planned – with faultless service, irresistible flavours and simply stunning presentation.

Fingers and Forks
SPICY SESAME TUNA TARTARE WITH WASABI CREAM

This crowd-pleasing recipe looks stunning decorated with red amaranth crispy spring onions and caviar, but is actually quite simple to put together. Buy the freshest sushi-grade tuna. Serves 4

Ingredients

For the tuna tartare:

360g tuna loin (sushi grade), finely diced

15ml toasted sesame oil

15ml Japanese soy sauce

2 tsp coriander, finely chopped

2 tsp pickled ginger, finely shredded

1 tsp hot red chilli, seeds removed and finely chopped (to taste)

1 clove garlic, crushed to a paste

1 tsp white sesame seeds

1 tsp black sesame seeds

For the wasabi cream:

120ml whipping cream

1 tsp wasabi paste, mixed with enough water to form a soft mixable paste (to taste)

1 tsp chives, finely chopped

Pinch salt

For the toppings:

4 tsp spring onions, finely shredded and fried crispy

4 tsp caviar (coloured flying fish roe for best effect)

4 pluches red amaranth or micro leaves

Method

For the tuna tartare, simply mix everything carefully together, taking care not to squash the tuna dice. Marinate, cover and place in the fridge for 20 minutes.

For the wasabi cream, carefully whip everything together until the mixture just holds its shape. Chill in the fridge for 10 minutes.

To serve, three-quarters fill double-size shot glasses or, for the brave, small ring moulds with the tuna tartare mixture. Top with the chilled wasabi cream mixture. Place a teaspoon of spring onion pieces in a pile carefully on top. Add the caviar next to the spring onions. Finish with red amaranth. Serve as part of a mixed starter plate or on its own as a lovely little pre-starter.

Henley
FOOD HEROES

Gabriel Machin has been at the heart of Henley-on-Thames for generations –
a traditional butchers that has gained a reputation for excellence throughout
Oxfordshire.

Nestled in the historic town centre of beautiful Henley-on-Thames, the traditional shop front of Gabriel Machin is a reminder of how long this renowned butchers has been standing as part of the local community. The original brick smoke house is one of very few still in use in the UK today, and they still smoke chicken, duck, bacon, salmon and eel on the premises – in fact Gabriel Machin receives a special mention in Rick Stein's Guide to the Food Heroes of Britain for their incredible smoked salmon.

For Barry Wagner, the owner, keeping traditions alive while moving into the 21st century is a fine balancing act, and one which is he is committed to maintain. He has worked at Gabriel Machin for 12 years and took the reins in 2015. Does he plan to make any changes to the 100-year-old business? "For me, it's about adding to the success, not changing anything," he says, as he is proud of its heritage but always striving to meet customers' needs and deliver the utmost in quality.

The tiny shop is an Aladdin's cave of goodies – locally sourced pork, award-winning sausages, the finest seasonal lamb, beef that has been dry-aged on the bone, game during the game season, home-cured bacon and salmon, a full fish counter, a mouth-watering selection of cheese… not to mention the oils, vinegars, spices and sauces that fill the shelves.

The queue regularly snakes outside the shop and the five members of staff greet each customer with a friendly smile and, quite often, customers are welcomed by name. The personal touch is part of the service here, and it's not just the locals who come back time after time, there are plenty of repeat customers who travel from far and wide to buy their meat at Gabriel Machin. Famous fans include Mary Berry and Antony Worrall Thompson, who uses their famous smoked salmon in his restaurant.

The knowledgeable staff know all there is to know about the provenance of their meat and are happy to answer questions about cooking techniques, recommend the perfect joint for the time you have available or offer advice on lesser known cuts. It doesn't matter how much or how little you are buying, the Gabriel Machin team love to share their passion with their valued customers.

Gabriel Machin's
BEEF CARBONNADE WITH HENLEY DARK ALE AND HORSERADISH DUMPLINGS

A full-flavoured beef and onion casserole, meltingly tender and served with light and delicate horseradish dumplings. Serves 4

Ingredients

1kg rump steak

1 carrot, very finely diced

2 sticks celery, very finely diced

2 cloves garlic, finely chopped

2 fresh bay leaves

3 stalks fresh thyme

2 tbsp plain flour

4 brown onions, sliced

2 tsp dark brown sugar

2 tsp wholegrain mustard

600ml Henley Dark Ale (or other dark but not too bitter ale)

Sunflower oil, for cooking

Salt and freshly ground black pepper

For the horseradish dumplings:

100g fresh white breadcrumbs

100g plain flour

100g shredded beef suet

1 tsp baking powder

A good pinch of flaked sea salt

1 heaped tsp strong creamed horseradish sauce

1 tbsp finely chopped parsley (optional)

2 eggs

Method

Preheat the oven to 160°C/fan 140°C/Gas 3.

Cut the steak into large even chunks. Cut the fat trimmings into small pieces. Set the meat aside.

Heat 1 tsp sunflower oil in a flameproof casserole pan. When the oil is hot, stir in the fat trimmings and sizzle without burning until they are brown and have released their oil. Remove the fat pieces from the pan and discard. Add the finely diced carrot and celery to the flavoured oil along with the garlic, bay leaves and the thyme. Stir well, put the lid on the pan and reduce the heat so that the vegetables can cook and soften while you prepare the meat. But do stir from time to time to make sure that the vegetables are not catching on the bottom of the pan.

Put the plain flour onto a flat dish and season well with salt and freshly ground black pepper. Put a heavy-based frying pan over a moderate heat and add 1 tbsp of sunflower oil. Working in batches, coat the rump steak pieces in the flour and fry until golden all over, then remove from the pan and set aside. Use the same oil to fry the onions (unless the flour and fat have burned, in which case wipe the pan clean and add a further tablespoon of oil and heat). Add the sliced onions to the pan and cook, stirring occasionally for about 10 minutes. Add the brown sugar and cook for a further 5 minutes, the onions should be a light golden brown. Stir in the mustard and the remains of the flour that you used to coat the rump steak in. Stir well. Pour in the ale, stirring well to ensure that your sauce is not lumpy. Bring to the boil and then remove from the heat.

The vegetables should now be soft and fragrant. Add the browned meat to the casserole and pour over the onion sauce, stirring gently to combine. Put a lid on the pan and cook in the oven for 2-2½ hours. The meat should be meltingly tender and the sauce thick and glossy.

25 minutes before the meat is cooked, make the dumplings. Bring a large pan of salted water to the boil. In a large bowl, mix the breadcrumbs, flour, suet, baking powder and salt. Break the eggs into a small bowl and mix with the horseradish sauce and the chopped parsley if using. Pour the eggs into the flour and mix gently to combine.

Flour a board and your hands. Divide the dough into 12 even pieces and shape into balls. Put the dumplings onto the floured board. Reduce the temperature under the pan so that the water is simmering. Cook the dumplings for about 10 minutes until they are risen and light.

Spoon the carbonnade into warm dishes and serve with the dumplings and carrot batons for an elegant and flavoursome meal.

Better BUTTER

Grant Harrington created Ampersand hand-crafted cultured butter with the sole aim of making the most buttery butter possible...

For chef Grant Harrington, butter became a bit of an obsession. Having worked at top restaurants in the UK including Maze by Gordon Ramsay, it was a move to the kitchens of Fäviken in Sweden that inspired Grant's journey into butter-making. There was something about the traditional butter in Sweden that he couldn't put his finger on. It was more 'buttery' than anything else he had ever tasted.

While in Sweden he set about learning why the ancient Scandinavian butter-making techniques produced something so full of flavour. He immersed himself into studying butter's fascinating history from ancient Arabia to the traditional fermentation techniques used in pre-industrialised Scandinavia. Full of enthusiasm and inspiration, he returned to the UK to continue his scientific research.

After a year of analysing, experimenting and investigating the different healthy bacteria that can be added to butter during the butter-making process (which also involved him building a cabin on a small dairy farm in Oxfordshire), Grant felt he had finally developed the most buttery butter possible.

His hand-crafted cultured butter is made using the finest Jersey cow's milk, famous for its creamy flavour, a healthy bacteria culture and mineral-rich Himalayan pink rock salt. Once the bacteria is added to the rich, yellow Jersey cream it is aged to perfect maturity before being churned. During this aging process, specific lactic acids are produced which are incredibly rich in buttery flavours. Finally, the unrefined pink rock salt is ground and hand-kneaded into the cultured butter.

The complex flavour – rich creaminess complemented by acidic buttery notes – has won over butter fans and plenty of famous foodies across Oxfordshire and the UK. Grant now supplies his butter to famous regional restaurants such as The Pointer in Brill, as well as some of the country's most celebrated restaurants, including Michelin-star Restaurant Story in London and two Michelin-star Restaurant Sat Bains in Nottingham.

If you want to buy it for your own kitchen, it is available from 2 North Parade in Oxford and Druid Street Market in London, and it is soon to be found in the fridges of Fortnum & Mason, too. With such interest in his unique British product, the next challenge for Grant will be keeping up with demand for his luxurious hand-crafted butter...

AMPERSAND
HAND CRAFTED
&
CULTURED BUTTER
UK ON 022 EC
HIMALAYAN ROCK SALT AND LACTIC CULTURES

Grant Harrington's

LEEKS COOKED OVER AN OPEN FIRE, ROAST TROUT & A SAUCE MADE FROM MELTED BUTTER, EGG YOLKS AND THE BURNT OUTER SHELL OF THE LEEKS

Serves 2

Ingredients

Good-quality charcoal

3 large leeks, carefully cleaned

500g cultured salted butter, melted

1 large fresh brown trout, cleaned*

2 large egg yolks

1 tsp Dijon mustard

200ml white wine vinegar (acidity more than 6%)

Groundnut oil

Additive-free salt**

Good bread and butter, to serve

---

* If you don't have the time for fishing, the brown trout you have sourced is most likely to have come from one of the UK's many trout farms, this isn't awful, to feed the world we live in today without farming, 99% of ingredients we enjoy wouldn't be sustainable. Aim for trout supplied from a farm where the fish can openly feed on natural aquatic insect life as well as their organic processed pellets.

** I prefer Himalayan rock salt for base seasoning as the earthy mineral flavours add mild bitter elements to the taste spectrum. I use Halen Mon sea salt when plating up to add a textural finish.

Method

Light the charcoal, but avoid using lighter fluids or any other similar chemicals which will taint the fire. Place a stainless steel bowl and fine sieve in the freezer. Trim the greenest tops off the leeks, and set the whole leeks aside. Make sure the leek tops are dry and then weigh them. Adding twice the mass of oil, blitz the ingredients whilst heating until the oil reaches 90°C. Immediately pass the oil through the chilled sieve into the chilled bowl and refrigerate until serving.

Using a very sharp knife and taking your time, thinly slice one leek into equal circles. Lay the leek circles so they all briefly overlap in a square, on top of a large piece of parchment paper. Lightly brush with melted butter and season with salt. Lightly grill the leek slices until they begin to go tender. Add another layer of parchment, refrigerate and compress the leek sheet between two flat surfaces until the butter and leeks have set. Portion the compressed leek in a shape that suits the service plate best, and reserve until plating.

Lightly salt the fish and set aside at room temperature until ready to cook.

With the lower roots attached, cook the other two leeks directly over the fire. Care for the vegetable as you would a good steak on a barbecue, ensuring each side receives equal amounts of direct heat. Once this is achieved, the outer shell of the leek will eventually be blackened and crisp, whilst the inner layers of the leek will be perfectly braised.

Remove the leeks from the fire and separate the burnt outer shell of the leek from the braised innards. Place the braised inner leeks on a preheated ceramic plate and rest in a warm area. To prevent the leeks from drying out, brush with hot melted butter regularly.

Place the burnt outer shells into a large container with the vinegar and ideally place in the fridge for 24 hours before straining the vinegar into sterilised glass bottles and storing in the fridge. If you're making it in on the day, blitz the leek ash in the vinegar and reserve the strained liquid.

Add a teaspoon of the filtered blitzed leek ash to the egg yolks, mustard and salt. Rapidly whisk together whilst slowly adding the groundnut oil (approximately 50g) and melted butter (approximately 200g), emulsifying the ingredients until they reach the consistency of a loose mayonnaise. Season to taste with additional salt and leek vinegar, enough to give it a good tang. Reserve for serving at room temperature.

Wipe the salt and excess moisture from the fish and place it on a stainless steel rack positioned upright (as if it were swimming). If the fish is wild and incredibly fresh, fillet and lightly torch the skin, before portioning and serving it almost raw. Alternatively, put the rack in a preheated oven at 190°C, until the fish is cooked rare; the core temperature of the fish should be almost (but not quite) body temperature. Carefully remove the fillets from the fish and immerse in the remaining butter in a warmed ceramic dish.

To plate the dish, quickly peel off the skin and cut the trout into pieces. Remove the outer tough layers of the leeks, and trim and portion in ratio to the plate size. Add the compressed leek shape to a warmed ceramic plate and dress the plate with leeks, fish, sauce, oil and vinegar.

Our HOUSE

After the recession hit, friends and colleagues Johnny Pugsley and Damion Farah weren't happy with the way the restaurant industry was headed, so they decided to go it alone.

Fast forward seven years and they've established the hugely successful House of Jacob, consisting of a delicatessen, two pubs and a chop house.

With 40 years of experience between them under their belts, the pair kicked things off with Jacobs & Field café/deli on Old High Street in Oxford. With a minimal budget most of the renovation work was done by themselves, with furniture reclaimed and upcycled from charity shops and even the odd skip!

Because they were a new, unknown business, Johnny and Damion expected to be able to run the whole operation as a duo; little did they know they would be packed to the rafters on their first day! After hiring a full team of staff the deli went from strength to strength, with their homemade fare (especially the breakfasts) hitting national industry press like Olive Magazine and Food and Travel.

Provenance is important in all aspects of the business so they strive to source ingredients as locally as possible and make everything in house where they can, from chutneys and jams to cakes, sausage rolls, ketchup and everything in between.

Next up came Jacob's Inn, which was an opportunity to really show what they could do. Making the most out of the huge garden area they built a pig pen so they could produce their own pork and space for chickens to provide the freshest eggs. The terrace area is purpose built for outdoor events like hog roasts and private parties; the popularity of these has not gone unnoticed and they were listed in GQ as one of the top 10 places to eat al fresco in the UK.

Jacob's Chop House followed, a relaxed style brasserie offering tasty cuts of meat and whole fish with which customers can choose their preferred sides, sauces and even wines and ales to match.

Their fourth offering comes in the form of The Woodstock Arms, which is similar to Jacob's Inn in that their food depends upon what they can get from local farms and producers. The menus change seasonally with daily specials to accommodate certain ingredients that may have grown in abundance nearby. Like its sister venues, The Woodstock has also been recognised as among the best in the industry, with a place in the Sawday's Guide and four AA stars for its five rooms.

Despite this whirlwind success, the team at The House Of Jacob are not resting on their laurels. They have recently bought the building behind the deli and have transformed it into an 80 seater restaurant with a pizza oven to cook up handmade stone baked sourdough pizzas.

Jacobs Chophouse
ROAST RIB OF BEEF

Ingredients

For the beef:

1 x 2.25 kg fore rib of beef (with 2 bones)

1 whole garlic bulb, broken into cloves

Small bunch of rosemary, leaves picked

Small bunch of thyme, leaves picked

Sea salt

Freshly ground black pepper

Olive oil

For the BEST roast potatoes!

1.5kg floury potatoes like Desiree or Rooster

1 tbsp semolina or flour

Goose fat

Sprig of fresh rosemary

1 tbsp salt

For the Yorkshire puddings:

2 large eggs

225ml milk

110g plain flour (4 heaped dessert spoons)

1-2 tbsp dripping or oil

Method

For the beef

Preheat the oven to 240°C. Take the beef out of the fridge 30 minutes before you want to cook it and allow it to come up to room temperature. Place a large sturdy roasting tray in the oven to heat up.

On a chopping board crush and chop 3 garlic cloves with the rosemary leaves, thyme, a pinch of sea salt, pepper and a glug of olive oil, then rub all over the beef.

Break up the remaining unpeeled garlic cloves and add to the hot roasting tray with the beef. Pop straight in the oven and roast for around 50 minutes, basting occasionally with the juices from the tray.

After 50 minutes, reduce the temperature to 190°C for around 10 minutes, or until the beef is beautifully golden brown on the outside and pink in the middle – leave in for longer if you prefer your beef well done.

Cover with tin foil and leave to rest for at least 20 minutes.

For the BEST roast potatoes!

Peel the potatoes and cut into quarters and halves.

Boil them in well-salted water until the outside of the potato is fluffy and done, then drain. Leave to dry in a sieve over the pan.

You can cook in the same oven as the beef at 190°C.

Put the goose fat in a roasting tin, big enough to take all of the potatoes in a single layer – you need enough fat to make a 1.5cm layer in the bottom of the tray.

Place in the oven to heat up, this needs to be very hot!

Give the sieve a good shake to rough up the potatoes a bit, mix with the semolina or flour and season.

Carefully add the potatoes to the hot fat, it should sizzle, then turn them until they are all coated in the goose fat. Chop the rosemary and sprinkle on top.

Roast for 20 minutes, then turn and roast for 20 minutes more, until crisp and golden.

For the Yorkshire puddings

The day before, blend all of the ingredients with a pinch of salt. Whizz until smooth then let the mixture rest overnight.

Heat the oven to 220°C.

Put the dripping or oil in one large tin or divide it between a muffin tin. Put it in the oven for ten minutes so the fat gets really hot.

Pour the batter into the tin and return to the middle of the oven.

Bake for 25 minutes, until very well risen and golden. Do not open the oven door until at least 20 minutes or they will sink.

Serve the beef with the roast potatoes, Yorkshire puddings, seasonal vegetables, gravy and horseradish.

Jacobs & Field

KING PRAWN AND CORIANDER PIZZA WITH SAN FRANCISCO SOURDOUGH

Ingredients

For the dough (enough for 5 large pizzas):

300ml sourdough starter (you can buy a variety of these online, we use a sixty year old San Francisco starter)

250ml warm water

300g Tipp Italian 00 flour

200g semolina flour

For the sauce:

2 tbsp olive oil

1 tbsp butter

170g onion, chopped

85g celery, chopped

1 garlic clove, minced

225g passata

170g tomato paste

2 tbsp Parmesan cheese, grated

1 tsp dried basil

1 tsp dried oregano

½ tsp salt

½ tsp sugar

¼ tsp black pepper

1 small bay leaf

1 tsp fennel seed

For the topping:

3 tbsp mozzarella, grated

3 tbsp Parmesan, finely grated

5 sun blushed tomatoes, halved

6 large Gambas (frozen and defrosted is fine), patted dry, deveined and butterflied

1 bunch of coriander, roughly chopped

Generous pinch chilli flakes

Handful pitted green olives, halved (or use capers)

Small drizzle extra virgin olive oil

Method

To make the sourdough

Weigh the ingredients into a mixing bowl and mix into a rough dough.

Knead the dough until smooth stretchy and soft. Then cover with cling film and allow to rest for 30 minutes.

Divide into five equal pieces and shape into rounds and cover. Rest for a couple of minutes.

One at a time, roll (or throw them) to make a delicious thin pizza base.

To make the sauce

In a large pan, melt butter with the oil. Add the onion, celery and garlic and sauté until soft and transparent. Add the passata and tomato paste and stir until smooth.

Add remaining ingredients and bring to a slow simmer.

Simmer for 45-60 minutes, remove the bay leaf and leave to cool.

To build

Put your pizza base into a pizza tray or large baking tray. Spread a ladle of the tomato sauce over the pizza base, leaving an inch around the edge.

Sprinkle on the mozzarella, place the Gambas around the pizza at uniform intervals of a clock face.

Spread the rest of the toppings randomly over the pizza and add a sprinkling of the Parmesan cheese.

Place in a hot oven for 8-10 minutes, until the cheese is bubbling and the Gambas are cooked through. Drizzle over olive oil and serve.

Jacobs Inn

ROAST CORNISH HAKE WITH CRAB AND HERB CRUST, PARMESAN POLENTA CHIPS, DILL AND SAFFRON CREAM SAUCE

Ingredients

4 x 170g pieces of fresh, boneless hake fillet

For the herb crust:

300g white crab meat

150g fresh white breadcrumbs

1 lemon, juice and finely grated zest

75g butter, melted

4 sprigs tarragon leaves, chopped

2 tbsp chives, chopped

½ tbsp parsley, finely chopped

For the polenta chips:

450ml water

125g polenta

Sprig of fresh rosemary

75g grated Parmesan cheese

½ tsp salt

For the dill and saffron cream sauce:

25g butter

75g shallot, finely chopped

2 garlic cloves, minced

450ml double cream

1 lemon, juice

¼ bunch dill, chopped

1 pinch saffron

Salt and pepper

Method

Preheat the oven to 180°C.

Mix all of the herb crust ingredients and press onto the hake fillets.

Roast the hake fillets for 12-15 minutes until golden and cooked through.

For the polenta chips

Boil the water then add the polenta and cook for 20 minutes.

Lower the heat and cook for 5 more minutes.

Spread the polenta in a tray lined with greaseproof paper to the desired thickness and allow to cool.

Cut into chips then roll in some dried polenta.

In oil, deep fry the polenta pieces for 4-5 minutes, adding the rosemary in for the last 20 seconds.

Drain and pat dry before sprinkling with the Parmesan and salt.

For the dill and saffron cream sauce

Melt the butter over a medium heat and cook the shallots and garlic until soft.

Add the cream and lemon juice.

Raise the heat and cook until reduced by a third and it has the consistency to coat the back of a spoon.

Add the dill, saffron and season to taste.

The Woodstock Arms

SLOW ROAST OXFORDSHIRE PORK BELLY WITH QUINCE AND PINE NUT STUFFING, FONDANT POTATO, BUTTERED GREENS AND MUSTARD SAUCE

Ingredients

For the roast pork:

2 tbsp fennel seeds

1 tbsp black peppercorns

Sea salt

2 lemons, juiced and zest

1 bunch thyme, chopped

3 garlic cloves, crushed

100ml olive oil

2.5kg free-range pork belly, boned and rolled

For the fondant potato:

150g butter

4 potatoes cut into barrel shapes

75ml vegetable or meat stock

Salt and pepper

2 garlic cloves, crushed

¼ bunch thyme

For the mustard sauce:

2 shallots, finally chopped

150ml white wine

1 bay leaf

2 tsp brown sugar

2 tbsp English mustard

1 tbsp wholegrain mustard

200ml crème fraîche

Method

Toast the fennel seeds and peppercorns and blend in a pestle and mortar with a pinch of sea salt, the lemon juice, zest, thyme and garlic to make a paste. Mix with olive oil and rub over the pork, then leave overnight to infuse.

Preheat the oven to 200°C.

Sit the pork on a wire rack in a roasting tin and cook for 30 minutes.

Turn down heat to 180°C and cook for a further 2 hours.

Bring the heat back up to 220°C and cook for 30 minutes to crisp up the crackling.

Rest for 20 minutes before slicing and serving.

For the fondant potato

Heat the butter over a medium heat in a saucepan.

When the butter is foaming add the potatoes and fry for 5-6 minutes on both sides until golden.

Pour in the stock, add a pinch of salt and pepper then the garlic and thyme. Cover with a lid and cook the potatoes until tender.

For the mustard sauce

Put shallots, wine, bay leaf and sugar in a pan over a medium heat, then simmer and reduce by half. Stir in the crème fraîche and mustard.

Kat Orman

LEMON AND ROSEMARY CHAR-GRILLED SPATCH COCK POUSSIN, SALSA VERDE, PEARL BARLEY, WATERCRESS, ASPARAGUS AND CRÈME FRAÎCHE

BBC Radio Oxford Mid-morning presenter Kat Orman shares her recipe for the perfect dinner. Light, fresh and full of flavour, this dish is ideal for impressing dinner party guests in spring when British asparagus is in season. Serves 4

Ingredients

4 spatchcock poussin's

400g pearl barley

12 asparagus spears, woody ends removed

250g tub of crème fraiche

Watercress, to garnish

For the marinade:

Olive oil

2 garlic cloves, sliced and peeled

1 lemon

Rosemary, finely chopped

Salt and pepper

For the salsa verde:

2 large gherkins, finely chopped

2 tbsp surfine capers, finely chopped

1 banana shallot, finely chopped

1 bunch flat leaf parsley, finely chopped

¼ bunch mint, finely chopped

½ bunch basil, finely chopped

1 lemon, juice and grated rind

1 tsp Dijon mustard

6 tbsp olive oil

Method

Ask the butcher to spatchcock the chickens for you. He will split them down the backbone and flatten them. When butchered this way, it allows for the marinade to penetrate the chicken fully as well as allowing for an even cook when chargrilled.

Place your chicken flat in a shallow dish. Liberally pour olive oil over the birds so that they are well coated, and then to this add sliced garlic, the juice and rind of a lemon, finely chopped rosemary and salt and pepper. Cover, place in the fridge and leave the chicken to marinate for at least a few hours.

To make the salsa verde

Mix the finely chopped gherkins, capers, shallots and herbs with the lemon juice, mustard and olive oil. The joy of this salsa is it can be made in advance and will last in your fridge for up to a week and is a great accompaniment to fish or chicken.

When your poussin's have marinated for the desired length of time place the birds skin-side down on a medium to low heated griddle pan. The idea is to allow the chicken to cook through without burning the skin, whilst retaining the wonderful taste and aesthetics of the griddle pan. A medium poussin should take 20–25 minutes to cook. Once cooked allow your poussin's to rest before serving.

In a saucepan cook your pearl barley in salted boiling water according to the packet instructions. When the grain is cooked to your liking, strain, add back to the pan and stir in your salsa verde. Blanch the asparagus.

To serve

Divide your pearl barley and salsa verde mixture between the plates along with your blanched asparagus. Place a poussin on top of each portion and garnish with watercress and a healthy dollop of crème fraîche.

Weekends start at
THE KITCHEN

The Kitchen at Farnborough is a newly refurbished and rebranded country eating house with a fresh vision for relaxed, rural dining; serving seasonal food cooked with love and care.

As The Inn at Farnborough, it was always popular for destination dining, but owners Jo and Anthony Robinson were striving for something new, wanting to make their own, slightly different mark on the country eating scene.

It all started when Jo and Anthony had the idea of creating their own kitchen garden, with an in-house gardener to nurture the quality and productivity they'd need. Plans for cultivating specific and seasonal vegetables, herbs and edible flowers were hatched and their whole new approach just grew from there.

After major investment in renovation, restoration and rebranding, plus a complete menu overhaul, and with an entirely new kitchen and front of house team, The Kitchen at Farnborough was born.

The focus at The Kitchen is all about creating exciting food by being selective and discerning about the ingredients used. Everything is freshly prepared in-house; championing local food heroes as much as possible. They use The Lost Farm at Grandborough (just 15 miles away) for rare breeds of meat such as Beef Shorthorn, Aberdeen Angus and Highland Cattle, as well as Tamworth and Gloucester Old Spot pork and a wonderful range of poultry; which feature on the ever-changing seasonal menus alongside vegetarian dishes and game, when in season too.

The drinks menus are equally inspiring, combining award-winning brands such as Cotswolds Gin and Chase Vodka with premium local ales and a fantastic wine list personally selected by Jo and Anthony.

They've also upped the ante when it comes to outdoor dining, with a wood fired pizza oven and plans to develop a fire pit so they can do all of their own smoking.

With plenty of outdoor space, The Kitchen isn't just dog friendly, it's positively encouraged. One look at their website and you'll find recommendations of local walks in the surrounding rolling countryside and National Trust village, meaning the whole family can join you on your weekend outing.

And that's what's embraced here, the concept of the long lazy weekend, even during the week! As Jo says: "There's nothing quite like sharing a great dinner around a table with family and friends. We're all about high quality food in a friendly, relaxed environment."

Focusing on being fiercely independent, it's clear owners Jo and Anthony have poured their hearts and souls into creating this popular foodie hub.

KITCHEN

RUSTIC BRITISH COOKING

The Kitchen Farnborough
ROAST COTSWOLD WHITE CHICKEN, HERB POTATO DUMPLINGS, BABY VEGETABLES, SAFFRON BROTH

Serves 4

Ingredients

For the chicken:

100g unsalted butter, softened

½ bunch of basil, finely shredded

Sea salt and fresh pepper

50ml extra virgin olive oil

1 medium sized whole Cotswold white chicken

1 litre good chicken stock

Pinch of saffron strands or 1 tsp powdered saffron

Baby seasonal vegetables e.g. asparagus, carrots, peas, turnips, cherry tomatoes

For the potato dumplings:

500g starchy potatoes, baked in their skins and still warm

1 small free-range egg, lightly beaten

Pinch of salt

160g plain flour

2 tbsp fresh tarragon and rosemary

Method

Preheat the oven to 180°C.

Mix the butter with the shredded basil and season with salt and pepper. Refrigerate half the basil butter.

Take the remaining half of the basil butter and push it under the skin of the chicken, being careful not to tear the skin.

Rub the chicken with olive oil and season with salt and pepper. Roast for approximately 1½ hours or until thoroughly cooked. When cooked remove from the oven and allow to rest in a warm place for 20 minutes.

Whilst the chicken is roasting, make the dumplings. Peel the potatoes and pass through a sieve. Place in a bowl, make a well in the centre, add the egg, salt and ¾ of the flour and the chopped herbs. Mix well to a dough consistency adding more flour if required.

Lightly dust a work surface with flour then roll out the dough into long cylinders, approximately 1-2cm wide. Cut the cylinders into little dumplings approximately 1-2cm in length. Place onto a flour dusted plate ensuring they are all kept separately, then refrigerate until required.

To serve

Whilst the chicken is resting, heat the stock and reduce to approximately half of the quantity. Add the saffron and allow to simmer.

Add the vegetables to the stock to cook, then add the dumplings 5 minutes before serving.

Joint the chicken into required pieces, then place in a serving dish and reheat for a few minutes in the oven.

Add the remaining basil butter to the simmering saffron stock to lightly thicken. Pour the stock and vegetables over the chicken, garnish with freshly picked garden herbs.

COUNTRY
EATING HOUSE

The Kitchen Farnborough
GARDEN RHUBARB, STRAWBERRIES AND CUSTARD

Serves 4

Ingredients

For the rhubarb and strawberries:

8 sticks of garden rhubarb, cut into 3cm pieces

200g strawberries, sliced

100ml water

250g caster sugar

50g fresh ginger

50ml grenadine syrup

3 gelatine leaves

15 mint leaves, chopped

15 basil leaves, chopped

For the custard:

4 large egg yolks

65g caster sugar

25g plain flour (sieved with the cornflour)

2 tsp cornflour

250ml milk

Half a vanilla pod, split

Ideas for garnishes (optional):

Strawberry sorbet

Toasted almonds, coconut and pistachios

Garden herbs and flowers

Method

For the rhubarb and strawberries

Preheat the oven to 180°C.

Place the rhubarb and strawberries on a baking tray and pour over the water. Sprinkle over the sugar, ginger and grenadine syrup and cover with tin foil. Bake in the oven for 10–15 minutes until just tender.

Meanwhile, soak the gelatine in a little cold water.

Remove the tray from the oven and allow to cool. Discard the ginger. Once the rhubarb has cooled, strain the liquid into a saucepan, bring to the boil and reduce over a gentle heat. It needs to be a syrup-like consistency that will heavily coat the back of a spoon.

Remove the gelatine from the water and melt in the syrup whilst stirring constantly. Allow to cool. Mix gently with the rhubarb and strawberry mix, finally add the chopped basil and mint leaves.

For the custard

Whisk together the egg yolks and sugar thoroughly. Add the flours and whisk until combined. Bring the milk to the boil with the vanilla pod, then strain into the egg mix, whisking continuously.

Return the custard to the pan and cook over a low to moderate heat for approximately 5 minutes, stirring constantly with a wooden spoon. As it thickens take off the heat when the consistency coats the back of a spoon. Pour the cooked custard mix into a bowl and cover with cling film to prevent a skin forming. Leave to cool in the fridge.

To serve

Spoon the rhubarb and strawberry mix into a glass followed by the custard, repeat to form layers finishing with custard.

Spoon over a little of the reserved syrup and top with the garnishes of your choice. We recommend sorbet sprinkled with nuts, garden herbs and flowers.

The MILLER'S TALE

After meeting in France back in 2001 Mary and Nick Galer honed their trade at a number of pubs, top restaurants and hotels before turning their hand to the historic Miller of Mansfield in Goring.

Since returning home Nick and Mary have been inspired by the French way of life. It's not just about the cuisine; the idea of leisurely time around the dinner table with great food and good company has fuelled their dream of opening their own place with that ethos at the heart of it.

And their past experiences have more than prepared them for the challenge. Both had stints at Heston Blumenthal's The Fat Duck Group, Mary at the Hinds Head and Nick as head chef at The Crown. You may also have seen them at The Goose (now The Red Lion), the Fleur de Lys in Dorchester or even at the Crazy Bear Farm Shop where they spent time learning butchery skills. All of this has equipped them for the task of renovating the historic building and creating an inspiring menu.

While it was the hotel side of the business that sustained them in their first year, word of mouth soon travelled. With their loyal suppliers following them to their new venture, their exciting seasonal à la carte menus, lunches and dinner clubs soon became the talk of the town and the monthly locals tasting night is now booked up four months in advance.

The food at The Miller embraces the quality of the raw produce as the most important thing, aiming to provide an experience that you can't recreate at home. Using interesting cuts and maximising exciting flavours, it's all about balance.

Whilst you can get a high end cut of steak, there's also ling, skate, shoulder of pork or more wholly unusual cuts like chicken cocks comb.

Their drinks menu is just as extensive. Cocktails are often staff preferences, you'll find local real ale on draught and their wine list has been personally tasted and selected, each bottle with a story behind it.

At The Miller of Mansfield everyone is catered for, whether you want to pop in for a pint, are having a couple of nibbles at the bar or if you're sampling their wine with a tasting flight alongside a five course dinner; you can sit wherever you want and choose from whichever menu takes your fancy. Nick, Mary and the staff at The Miller strive to accommodate all in a friendly, welcoming environment – so it's no wonder this already decorated business (two AA rosettes and four stars) has continued to earn its stripes by being awarded Restaurant of the Year in the Waitrose Good Food Guide 2016.

Miller of Mansfield

WILTSHIRE HOGGET LAMB, CONFIT ONION, JERUSALEM ARTICHOKE PURÉE AND HOT POT

Ingredients

Method

Serves 8

For the hot pot lamb ragu:

100g lamb fat

500g lamb mince

1 large donkey carrot, diced

5 white onions, diced

2 star anise

¼ bunch thyme

1 white leek, diced

1½ cloves of garlic, sliced

10g tomato purée

250ml red wine

200ml water

200ml reduced beef stock

10g Dijon mustard

15ml red wine vinegar

10ml Worcestershire sauce

For the lamb loin:

1 lamb loin (saddle) from a good butcher

300ml olive oil

10g thyme

10g rosemary

Salt

For the lamb sauce:

80g unsalted butter

80ml olive oil

1kg minced lamb shoulder (or minced lamb)

500g carrots, sliced

500g onions, sliced

5g whole star anise

750ml water cold

Good quality red wine vinegar, lamb fat and rosemary oil, to season

For the mint oil:

2 bunches of mint (to give 200g blanched mint)

200ml vegetable oil

For the mint vinaigrette:

250ml mint oil (from above)

20ml Chardonnay vinegar

For the savoy cabbage with chive:

1 large savoy cabbage, finely shredded

5g finely chopped chives

20g garlic butter

2 litres water

Salt

For the red cabbage purée:

1 jar of pickled red cabbage

For the confit baby white onions:

6 baby white onions, peeled whole

100g lamb fat, melted

For the hot pot lamb ragu

Place a large pan over a high heat and begin to brown the mince in batches in the lamb fat. Reserve the mince and fat for later use. Do not clean the pan.

Place the carrot and onion into the pan with some lamb fat and sweat for 5 minutes.

Tie the star anise and thyme in a muslin bag.

Add the leek, garlic, star anise and thyme.

Sweat for further 10-15 minutes.

Add the tomato purée and stir in and cook for 2 minutes.

Add the red wine and reduce to a syrup.

Add the cooked lamb mince back into the mix and add the water and reduced beef stock.

Bring to the boil and reduce into the ragu.

When the liquid has reduced finish with the Dijon mustard, red wine vinegar, and Worcestershire sauce.

Cook for a further 5-10 minutes until thick and glossy.

Cool as quickly as possible in a large container.

Reserve until ready to portion and reheat.

For the lamb loin

Preheat the oven to 200°C. Place the loin into a large container with the olive oil, thyme and rosemary and marinate for 4 hours in the fridge.

When needed, remove from the marinade pat dry with kitchen cloth. Season with fine and coarse salt.

Place into a hot pan with some lamb fat and brown off until golden brown on all sides.

Place into the oven for 3 minutes and then remove and rest for 5 minutes. Carve and serve.

For the lamb sauce

Place half the butter and oil into a large saucepan and wait for the butter to foam.

Add the minced lamb shoulder and cook until dark golden brown.

Remove the lamb from the pan and set aside.

Add the other half of the butter, oil and add the carrots and sweat until soft, stirring occasionally. Once the carrots are soft, add the onions, star anise and continue to cook until the onions are soft.

Return the seared lamb to the pan and stir so the meat and vegetables are thoroughly incorporated.

Add the water and bring to the boil, skimming off any impurities that rise to the surface. Simmer and keep skimming impurities for 4 hours.

After 4 hours, remove from the heat and allow to stand for 10 minutes before passing through a double muslin cloth.

Chill as quickly as possible.

Once chilled, remove the fat from the top and reserve.

Place the stock into another saucepan and reduce over a controlled heat. Skim to remove the impurities when necessary.

Reduce the sauce for taste and consistency.

Season with good quality red wine vinegar, lamb fat and rosemary oil.

Once reduced and finished, chill as quickly as possible.

For the mint oil

Blanch the mint in boiling water for 20 seconds. Cool in iced water.

Squeeze the excess moisture out then dry between paper towels.

Place in a powerful blender and blitz with the oil until smooth.

Drip through a tea towel overnight in the fridge.

For the mint vinaigrette

Emulsify the oil and vinegar together in a bottle and reserve for service.

For the savoy cabbage with chive

Boil the water and add a good pinch of salt.

Place the cabbage in batches into the boiling water for 30 seconds and then plunge directly into iced water to stop the cooking process.

Ring the water from the cabbage and dry on tea towels.

When you are ready to cook, place the garlic butter into a medium heat saucepan and then add the cabbage, lightly fry and season with salt.

Add in the chopped chives and serve.

For the red cabbage purée

Separate the pickling liquid and red cabbage.

Place the red cabbage into a food processor and blitz on full for 1 minute.

To get a nice purée consistency, use the reserved pickling liquid to loosen the red cabbage.

Serve the purée cold.

For the confit baby white onions

Place the baby onions into a medium saucepan and add the lamb fat.

Place over a low heat and slowly confit for 2 hours.

Remove the pan from the heat and allow the onion to cool naturally.

Slice the onions in half and fry the open side in a hot frying pan until dark golden brown.

Serve.

Like a
DUCK TO WATER

The Muddy Duck has put the village idyll of Hethe on the rural gastronomic map, breathing new life into its historic foundations and drawing in the crowds with its delicious dishes.

The family-owned, independent pub The Muddy Duck was born from a shared passion to challenge the restaurant scene, taking classic dishes and giving them a current but no-fancy-pants twist, while upping the ante on customer service and experience. Refreshingly, whilst they take the job in hand seriously, the atmosphere is relaxed and personable, and is always topped with a generous dollop of humour.

The resulting Muddy Duck is slickly delivered, but neither bland nor scripted, and it is this self-branded "two-faced" approach which has attracted a legion of loyal regulars.

The pub itself is an Aladdin's cave with areas to suit all seasons and moods – the pub is a snug of tartan, waxed oak and roaring hearth, bringing together a charming mix of locals, pre-dinner drinkers and impromptu family gatherings.

Whilst still being relaxed and honest, the barn-style Malthouse restaurant gives a buzzing sense of occasion. On fair days, the dining terrace provides an extension of the restaurant. Nestled under giant heated parasols, al fresco dining can be pushed well into the autumn, assisted by the novel trunk of Arran rugs, which are welcomed by diners who want to enjoy the outdoors on cooler evenings. The quirky beer garden and wooded copse, which holds host to legendary Oxfordshire pub favourite Aunt Sally, is a great spot to indulge in The Muddy Duck's legendary nibbles – including the amazing foot-long pork crackling sticks!

When the team at The Muddy Duck roll out the well-used line, "we're passionate about food", you can be sure they're not talking cobblers. Delivering quality products and encouraging a sense of community around that ethos runs in the owners' blood. They've spent their working careers promoting better food, be it in wholesale, retail or catering.

This dedication means quality is never compromised at The Muddy Duck and, in a bid to encourage locals out of the supermarkets and to support British, high-welfare, sustainable producers, The Duck's Pantry provides a charming seasonal, roving food market where people can pick up all their fresh weekly essentials. The Duck's Pantry often takes up residence on local farms – championing the true meaning of "field fresh".

The Muddy Duck

QUACK!

OPEN Daily

MONDAY – FRIDAY 9.30
SATURDAY 9.30
SUNDAY 10

The Muddy Duck
DUCK AND BACON SALAD

You can also serve this delicious salad as a starter, in which case it will serve 8 people. We use Tidenham, Cotswold duck at The Muddy Duck. Serves 4

Ingredients

For the duck confit:

4 large English duck legs, bone in

1 orange

2 cinnamon sticks

4 star anise

1 thumb-sized piece of root ginger, chopped, skin on and washed

1 lemon grass stick, bashed

2 sprigs rosemary

1 large red chilli, split lengthways

250ml vegetable oil

For the salad:

Hoisin sauce (in the pub we use a spiced homemade plum and ginger sauce, though a shop brought hoisin will work fine)

A mix of interesting salad and herb leaves (e.g. watercress, pea shoot, coriander leaf, chicory, baby spinach)

Pickled cucumber, skin off, sliced or diced (we pickle this in rice wine vinegar, ginger, garlic, salt and sugar)

A few spring onions, sliced

A few slices of crispy smoked streaky bacon

Method

Preheat the oven to 160°C.

Place the duck legs in an ovenproof dish, cut the orange into quarters and place in with the duck legs along with all of the other ingredients. The oil should just be up to the top of the duck legs, not quite covering.

Tightly cover the top of the dish with tin foil and place in the preheated oven for approximately 1 hour 30 minutes.

Remove from the oven, allow to cool a little, then remove the duck legs from the confit oil. The meat should be succulent, flaking into pieces and falling from the bone. In the pub kitchen we then remove the skin and just keep the meat, though it's up to you if you choose to crisp up the skin, as this is delicious!

The duck meat is now ready to crisp up to use immediately or can be cooled down completely and refrigerated to use another day.

To prepare the salad, in a hot pan (or in a hot oven) heat up and crisp the flaked duck leg meat. The meat should start to go all crispy around the outside, with a lovely soft centre. When the meat is hot and crisp, add a small amount of hoisin to coat the crispy meat.

In the pub we would then serve this as an individual plated salad, though at home this is great served as bowls of crispy hoisin duck and lovely herby cucumber and spring onion salad for your friends to dig into. Simply mix up the salad ingredients and serve.

The Muddy Duck
FISH STEW

The stew can be adjusted to use all types of shellfish and seafood. We always use sustainably caught seafood that is supplied through St Ives, Cornwall and Brixham in Devon. Serves 4

Ingredients

20 mussels

16 clams

50g chopped shallots

10g garlic purée

10g fennel seeds

½ long red chilli (dependent on heat)

A splash of white wine (pick one that goes well with your lunch)

500g tomato and basil passata (thick good-quality tomato sauce)

100g smoked haddock trimmings

50g brown shrimp

100g peeled prawns or cooked, peeled king prawns

2 sea bass fillets, cut into 4 pieces

100g squid, cleaned, scored and sliced

20g basil, chopped

50g saffron aioli, to serve

4 slices toasted garlic ciabatta, to serve

Extra virgin olive oil, to drizzle

Salt and pepper

Method

Into a hot saucepan add the mussels and clams with the shallots, garlic, fennel seeds, chilli and a little white wine. Place a lid on the pan and allow the shellfish to open up.

Once the shells are open (discard any that have not opened) add the tomato sauce and the smoked haddock, shrimp and prawns. Bring to a simmer to cook the fish.

Whilst the sauce is cooking, in a separate pan, pan-fry the fillets of sea bass, cooking them skin-side down, and season with milled black pepper and sea salt. Depending on the thickness of the fillets cook for a couple of minutes, then, in the last minute of cooking, add the squid to the hot pan to cook through.

To finish the sauce, add chopped basil. Divide the sauce and shellfish equally between four large bowls, place the open shells and prawns on the dishes so they present nicely, then place the sea bass fillets and squid on top. Decorate with saffron aioli and serve with toasted garlic ciabatta.

The Muddy Duck
STICKY TOFFEE 'BOCKERGLORY'

This is a bit of fun, though very popular – especially in the summer, with the old school retro style knickerbockers bringing back childhood memories!

Serves 10

Ingredients

Homemade sticky toffee sponge, cut into 2cm pieces (see below)

Caramel sauce (see below)

Sweet and salty caramel popcorn (see below)

Vanilla or honeycomb ice cream

British raspberries (with a squeeze of lime juice and icing sugar, if you like)

Thick double cream, whipped

Mint sprigs

For the homemade sticky toffee sponge:

400g chopped dates

350g boiling water

200ml milk

175g black treacle

170g butter

280g Demerara sugar

4 free-range eggs

1 tsp vanilla paste

1.4kg self-raising flour, sifted

2 tsp bicarbonate of soda

For the caramel sauce:

250g dark molasses or dark brown sugar

250g butter

250g double cream

For the sweet and salty popcorn:

50g popping corn

150g sugar

40g butter

5g sea salt

Method

To make the sticky toffee sponge, preheat the oven to 165°C. In a saucepan boil the chopped dates and water until the date mix is soft and the water is absorbed. Leave aside to cool. Separately warm the milk and treacle. Beat together the butter and sugar until thick, then gradually add the eggs one at a time, followed by the vanilla paste. Fold in the sieved flour, then add the bicarbonate of soda to the warm date mix. Fold the date mix into the butter and flour, then do the same with the warmed milk and treacle. Pour the mix into a parchment-lined dish and bake for approximately 35 minutes.

For the caramel sauce, place all the ingredients together in a pan, carefully bring to the boil and reduce to a thick pouring consistency.

For the popcorn, prepare a tray with greaseproof paper. Put the popping corn in a microwave. Make the caramel by melting the sugar in a pan, lower the heat and add the butter. Stir quickly until the butter emulsifies. Add the popped corn and stir to evenly coat. Spread the popcorn out on the lined tray and sprinkle with the salt.

To build the dish, in the base of glass add marinated raspberries, then build on top, layer by layer using the ice cream, cream and warm sticky toffee pudding and hot caramel sauce. Garnish with popcorn and mint sprigs. Get stuck in immediately!

Delicious, NATURALLY

For hand-crafted artisan bread made completely naturally with locally milled flour – Natural Bread have got it covered...

Natural Bread is a family business through and through. Growing up in France, Claire Véry was surrounded by a love of food from an early age. She recalls her fondness for the local markets, packed with vibrant colours of vegetables and the irresistible aromas of freshly baked bread. Her husband William Black shared her passion for natural homemade food and in particular for making bread without any additives or preservatives.

In 2006 they set up Appleton Farmers Market, having realised that there wasn't a market locally to rival the markets Claire had loved in France. With nobody offering fresh bread in the area, they set about perfecting their own sourdough recipe. William gathered every book he could find on sourdough and travelled across Europe to seek inspiration from bakers in France, Italy and beyond. Sourdough's are naturally leavened, using traditional slow fermentation techniques, which creates a distinctive and delicious fresh loaf that also keeps well for a few days.

Their homemade sourdough was introduced to the food enthusiasts of Oxfordshire at Appleton Farmers Market. Almost immediately they were selling out completely every market day and soon couldn't keep up with production in their home kitchen. A pizza oven in their garage was brought back to life to keep up with the ever-increasing demand, until they moved to a commercial bakery in Botley.

The first Natural Bread shop and café was soon opened in Eynsham in 2008, followed by an additional shop and café in Woodstock in 2009 and the flagship premises in Oxford's Little Clarendon Street in 2013. Add to that a successful wholesale business supplying breads and cakes to restaurants and cafés across Oxfordshire and life became very busy for Claire and William.

Sadly, William Black passed away on December 7th 2014, following a year-long battle with a brain tumour. Determined to continue with the vision that had inspired him, Claire has kept William's love of good food, natural ingredients and family values at the heart of Natural Bread. With her three daughters sharing the family passion for baking, there is hope and excitement for the future of the family business. The oldest, Charlotte, manages the Oxford store, 17-year-old Georgia is currently a trainee and 12-year-old Lola is a whizz in the kitchen too – clearly sharing her father's skills for making bread!

Today the range includes all sorts of loaves, buns, cakes, pastries and Viennoiserie – and you can see from the variety how the team are inspired by their travels around the world. Brunch, lunch, sandwiches and single-estate coffee and teas are also on offer. Whatever you choose from Natural Bread, it is always 100% natural and 100% delicious.

Natural Bread
A TWIST ON A CLASSIC BREAD PUDDING

This is a rich and indulgent recipe for using up leftover croissants – but it is so delicious, you could always buy some Natural Bread croissants especially for making it! Serves 15

Ingredients

200g butter

300g soft brown sugar

4 eggs

2 tsp mixed spice

1 tsp cinnamon

1 litre double cream

10 leftover croissants or slices of old bread, sliced in half

250g sultanas

15g Demerara sugar

Method

Preheat the oven to 160°C. Grease and line a baking tray.

Melt the butter and sugar in the microwave. Whisk the butter mixture into the eggs, then add the mixed spice and cinnamon and mix thoroughly. Pour in the cream and set aside.

Layer the croissants into the lined tray, alternating with the custard mixture and sultanas. Finish off with the Demerara sugar sprinkled on top.

Bake in the preheated oven for 50 minutes until the custard has set.

Michelin-starred
VILLAGE PUB

The Nut Tree Inn is a welcoming village inn at the heart of Otmoor, offering a friendly atmosphere and an award-winning dining experience, holding a Michelin star for an impressive eight years running.

Under the thatched roof of the grade II listed 15th-century building, Mike and Imogen North offer a warm welcome to every guest. The pub is an idyllic scene of picture-postcard perfection – an historic British inn which has stood in the village of Murcott for hundreds of years.

For Mike and Imogen, becoming proprietors of The Nut Tree Inn had always been a dream. Growing up in the area, Mike had known the charming pub his whole life and had always had a vision of what he could bring to the delightful premises. In 2006, when the opportunity arose to purchase the pub, Mike and Imogen didn't think twice, and their dream became a reality.

True to its heritage, The Nut Tree is a local village pub at its heart – it's a place where you can pop in and enjoy a relaxing drink at the end of the day or a pint in the sunshine on one of the picnic tables outside. However, what sets it apart from neighbouring watering holes is its award-winning restaurant which serves modern British food, perfectly executed.

Diners from around the country seek out the restaurant thanks to its remarkable reputation and string of accolades – alongside its Michelin star, The Nut Tree Inn has also won

awards for the 'best use of local produce' in the Waitrose Good Food Guide, Newcomer of the Year by Harden's, and a 'Catey' (the equivalent of an Oscar in the catering industry) as well as being voted one of the Top 50 Best Pubs in the UK since Mike and Imogen took the helm together.

From the faultless service and the enticing ambience to the accomplished cooking and impressive wine list, it is clear why this gustatory gem has become a favourite with local diners and critics alike. Seasonal and locally sourced ingredients are prepared with care and creativity, making the most of Oxfordshire's bountiful countryside – in fact the succulent pork sometimes comes from their own rare-breed pigs, and much of the produce used is grown in the kitchen gardens to the rear of the premises.

Whether you are going to The Nut Tree for a pint and a sandwich or an eight-course tasting menu with wine flight, you can rest assured that the welcome and quality will be the same.

The Nut Tree Inn
GINGER PANNA COTTA WITH YORKSHIRE RHUBARB

A truly stunning dessert from The Nut Tree Inn, which makes the most of beautiful pink Yorkshire rhubarb when it is available. Serves 4

Ingredients

For the panna cotta:

400ml double cream

100ml semi-skimmed milk

155g caster sugar

200g fresh ginger, chopped

2 leaves of gelatine

For the rhubarb:

4 sticks of Yorkshire rhubarb

200g caster sugar

1 split vanilla pod

1 star anise

For the rhubarb sherbet:

50ml semi-skimmed milk

50ml double cream

100ml of the rhubarb cooking juices

Lemon juice, to taste

Sugar, to taste

To garnish:

Pieces of meringue

Pieces of honeycomb

Mint, Thai basil or lemon verbena

Method

For the panna cotta

Mix the cream, milk, sugar and ginger in a pan and bring to the boil. Remove from the heat and leave to stand for 30 minutes to infuse, then strain. Soak the gelatine in cold water until soft. Add the gelatine to the warm mixture and stir until dissolved. Divide the mixture between 4 dariole moulds and place in the fridge to set for a minimum of 6 hours.

For the rhubarb

Preheat the oven to 180°C. Wash and cut the rhubarb into 7.5cm sticks. Place in an ovenproof dish or deep tray, sprinkle with sugar, vanilla pod and star anise. Cover with tin foil and bake in the preheated oven for approximately 8 minutes or until tender. Chill and reserve.

For the rhubarb sherbet

Mix the milk, cream and rhubarb syrup together and check taste for sweetness and acidity. Add lemon juice and sugar to taste, then churn in an ice cream machine. Place in the freezer until required.

To serve

Turn out the panna cotta by dropping in hot water and place slightly off centre on a round plate. Serve with the rhubarb batons, rhubarb juice and a scoop of rhubarb sherbet. We also garnish the dish with pieces of meringue, honeycomb and either mint, Thai basil or lemon verbena.

Welcome with
OPEN ARMS

The 19th-century pub and eating house The Oxford Arms wins over customers with its warm hospitality and cosy feel as soon as they step inside...

A traditional pub in the centre of the lovely village of Kirtlington, The Oxford Arms is recommended in The Good Pub Guide as a: "Civilised and friendly stripped-stone pub with enjoyable food and good wine choice."

The traditional feel runs through everything, from the large wood-burning stove which takes centre stage in the cosy interior to the no-nonsense approach to excellent dining that has won it acclaim from far and wide, including recommendations in The Good Food Guide and Alistair Sawday's, as well as The Good Pub Guide.

Chef patron Bryn Jones has been at the helm for over 12 years. A classically trained chef with many years of experience behind him, his focus is on "proper food" where everything is cooked fresh, on the premises and to the highest standards. Not one for following the latest fads, the ethos in his kitchen is to ensure dishes use local produce and are cooked to exacting standards – a philosophy that has seen The Oxford Arms become one of Oxfordshire's most popular dining pubs.

There is something for everyone here, from the hikers who stop by for a pint and potted shrimps or a tasty hand-crafted pork pie and homemade piccalilli, to diners who come to enjoy fine dining offerings such as grilled swordfish steak on warm caponata. There is an excellent wine cellar too, not to mention a notable selection of beers and whiskies.

Bryn is keen on taking inspiration from around the world and showcasing local ingredients at their heart, a dish such as their Rousham salt beef hash with fried duck eggs, lovingly made with Rousham rare-breed longhorn beef is a perfect example. The kitchen garden provides fresh fruits and vegetables, such as tomatoes (which are used in the homemade chutney) and courgettes.

They also hold a range of theme nights which bring the community together for an evening of fun. These range from Spanish nights to foraging evenings (wild garlic, mushrooms and blackberries have been popular choices) where the villagers will bring their foraged goodies back to The Oxford Arms to be whipped up into delicious dishes.

As well as locals who come regularly, The Oxford Arms attracts many diners who seek them out from across the county and even further afield. In the summer the huge and beautiful garden is an idyllic spot for dinner or a drink – as well as providing an incredible, flexible location for weddings and private functions. With the historic stone building, stunning outside space and top-quality food and service, there couldn't be a more perfect spot to hold a party.

The Oxford Arms

NATURAL SMOKED HADDOCK, LEEK AND CARAMELISED ONION TART

We have chosen this recipe because it's one of our most popular dishes and it's easy to repeat at home – no special skills required, only your heart and soul and love of food! The pastry is crisp and airy, and the filling is moist and tender.

Serves 6-8

Ingredients

For the pastry:

250g plain flour

125g butter, cubed

A pinch of salt

120ml cold water

For the filling:

1 medium fillet of natural smoked haddock

1 large onion, halved and thinly sliced

1 leek, shredded

3 eggs, beaten

¼ bunch of chives

400ml double cream

25g grated Parmesan or cheddar, to sprinkle

Butter and vegetable oil, for cooking

Salt and pepper

Method

For the pastry, sieve the flour into a bowl, add the butter and salt and rub with your fingers until the mixture becomes like breadcrumbs. Add the cold water slowly, a little at a time, and combine with the crumbs until you have a smooth pastry. Cover with cling film and place in the fridge for half an hour.

Preheat the oven to 200°C/400°F.

Place the haddock fillet on a baking tray, put a couple of knobs of butter on top of the fillet and cook in the hot oven for 10 minutes. Allow to cool, then remove the skin and flake the fish. Leave the oven on.

Cut the onion in half and slice thinly. Caramelise the onion (cook it very slowly) with some vegetable oil and butter in a pan set over low heat for approximately 20 minutes. Fry the shredded leeks in butter for 3 minutes, drain in a colander and set both aside.

Turn out the pastry onto a floured board and roll out to fill a 25cm flan ring that is about 3cm tall. Bake blind with baking beans for 20 minutes, then allow to cool. Leave the oven on.

Spread the onions the leeks onto the pastry base and flake the smoked haddock on top. Chop the chives into the eggs. In a saucepan bring the cream to the boil, then pour on to eggs and chives, whisk and immediately pour into the tart case on top of the leeks and onions. Sprinkle the grated Parmesan or cheddar on top.

Bake in the oven for approximately 35 minutes. If you don't have a conventional oven, rotate the tart every 10 minutes to ensure even cooking. Test with a knife to ensure the egg mixture is set, then allow to cool for at least 20 minutes before taking the tart out of the flan ring.

Say CHEESE

Situated in Oxford's covered market since 1986, The Oxford Cheese Company has been supplying quality local and continental cheeses to the people of Oxfordshire for 20 years.

Robert Pouget began selling cheese in Oxford's covered market in 1983, before forming The Oxford Cheese Company three years later. It may seem an unusual career choice for Baron Robert Pouget, who was – and still is – a talented artist and furniture designer. However, bringing the finest cheese to Oxford is something that he is incredibly passionate about, and this passion has seen his business go from strength to strength over the last two decades.

In 1995 Robert Pouget set his creative sights on producing his own semi-soft blue cheese for his shop. Having identified the lack of English blue cheeses to rival the popular European choices like Dolcelatte and Gorgonzola, he began to develop his own recipe. He worked alongside a Stilton manufacturer and, with their help and technical expertise, he produced his creamy semi-soft Oxford Blue.

In 2003, The Oxford Cheese Company began producing Oxford Isis, a washed-rind, full-fat soft cheese. It is washed in Oxfordshire Honey Mead and has a creamy consistency, pronounced flavour and floral aroma. This award-winning cheese quickly became a popular choice for cheeseboards across the county and further afield – it has been served at Royal Ascot and Wimbledon, and features on the menus of some of the country's top restaurants.

A lovely cheese for cooking with, as well as a favourite on cheeseboards, Oxford Isis features in The Oxford Cheese Company's take on a classic tartiflette overleaf – a perfect alternative to Reblochon. Always developing ideas and creating new products, Robert Pouget has also developed a complex and distinctive sauce, Oxford Sauce. The Baron's elusive fiery sauce has gained a cult following around the world, with orders coming in from London, Spain, America and even Australia!

Don't forget, however, The Oxford Cheese Company are home to many other cheeses, too, with some of the country's finest offerings on sale alongside some continental classics. The team are knowledgeable about their products and are always happy to offer advice and recommendations to customers.

One of their favourite services is creating incredible cheese wedding cakes for customers – beautiful stacks of cheese that can be selected to suit the number of guests and reflect the tastes of the couple. These show-stoppers make a perfect alternative to a traditional wedding cake and are sure to create a centrepiece to remember.

The Oxford Cheese Co.
ISISFLETTE

This is a take on the French alpine cheese and potato bake, tartiflette, which is very popular with the après ski fraternity. It uses Oxford Isis cheese instead of the traditional Reblochon. Serves 4

Ingredients

1kg potatoes

4 shallots, chopped

1 medium onion, chopped

1 clove garlic, chopped

250g lardons or chopped pork belly

150ml white wine

200g crème fraîche or double cream

2 whole Oxford Isis cheese (400g)

Salt and pepper

Sunflower oil

Method

Peel and boil the potatoes in salted boiling water for approximately 10 minutes until cooked (do not overcook). Drain the potatoes and set aside to cool.

Fry the shallots, onion, garlic and lardons in a little sunflower oil until browned and cooked and then add the white wine and continue to cook until the liquid has nearly evaporated.

Preheat the oven to 180-200°C.

Slice the potatoes thinly into an oven proof dish with the lardon and onion mix. Pour over the crème fraîche or cream. Sprinkle over a little salt and freshly ground pepper. Finally slice the two rounds of Isis horizontally to make four discs and lay them on the potatoes with the crusts upwards.

Bake in the oven for 10–15 minutes until the cheese crust topping is brown and bubbling. The cheese underneath will have melted into the potatoes.

Welcome to the
NEIGHBOURHOOD

A restaurant in the heart of Summertown that has certainly got people talking – critics and local foodies alike – The Oxford Kitchen is one of the most exciting eateries in Oxfordshire.

Since it launched in Oxford's Summertown in 2014, The Oxford Kitchen has quietly and quickly taken its place as one of the city's most celebrated restaurants. With rave reviews coming in thick and fast, 2015 saw this gustatory gem acquire two AA rosettes, as well as a TripAdvisor certificate of Excellence and awards from The Oxfordshire Restaurant Awards, The Food Awards England (where it was named Best Restaurant in the South of England) and Open Table Diners' Choice Awards.

The independent neighbourhood restaurant aims to offer fine dining without the fuss – an approach that has seen it become a firm favourite with locals who come to enjoy the culinary excellence of executive chef John Footman in the relaxed setting and comfortable atmosphere.

For John and his talented team, the focus of his kitchen is on providing the very best dishes and it's as simple as that. This means sourcing the finest quality ingredients and cooking them with skill and care, being creative with flavours and taking inspiration from around the world. Ultimately John attributes their success to striving for the best every single day.

Despite its success and recognition for fine dining excellence, there is no pretension at The Oxford Kitchen. The ambience is relaxed and informal and the accomplished front of house team welcome people inside with warmth and genuine hospitality.

An impressive wine list is available with carefully selected bottles covering a range of budgets and tastes. The helpful team can offer guidance on selecting the perfect bottle or you can opt for a uniquely delicious cocktail from the bar – their hugely popular Flower Power (elderflower cordial and lychee liqueur topped with Chapel Down Rose Champagne) makes a perfect aperitif!

The Oxford Kitchen
LAMB LOIN WITH TABOULE AND CONFIT BABY TOMATOES

Ingredients

300g lamb bones, chopped
20g butter

For the mirepoix:
30g carrot, 2cm dice
30g onion, 2cm dice
20g celery, 2cm dice
20g leek, 2cm dice

For the lamb:
200g lamb shoulder, diced 2 inches
20g butter
1 litre lamb remi/brown chicken stock
80ml white wine, reduced to 50ml
50g tomatoes, chopped
1 tsp thyme
Pinch of rosemary
1 tsp garlic, crushed

For the taboulé:
200ml water
1 tsp salt
15ml olive oil
200g couscous
1 tsp fennel seeds, soaked in warm water for 1 hour
40g pumpkin seeds (toast in a hot pan until golden brown)
40g pine kernels
40g raisins, soaked in warm water
10g parsley, fine julienne
10g coriander, fine julienne
60ml olive oil
30ml lemon juice
Pinch of cayenne pepper

For the confit tomatoes:
1kg baby plum tomatoes, blanched and peeled
100ml extra virgin olive oil
2 tsp thyme
1 tsp salt
1 tsp sugar
1 tsp pepper

Method

For the lamb

Sear the chopped bones over a strong heat until they just begin to colour. Add the butter and continue to cook in foaming butter for 10 minutes until nicely caramelised. Drain well.

In a separate pan, brown the mirepoix and drain well.

Slowly caramelise the diced lamb shoulder in the foaming butter. Drain well.

Bring the stock to the boil and reduce to sauce consistency.

Mix the remiage, white wine, bones, mirepoix and tomatoes. Bring to the boil, skim and simmer for 20 minutes.

Strain, reduce to sauce consistency. Refresh with caramelised shoulder, herbs and garlic.

Pass through a fine chinois, season and if too flat, add a little reduced white wine or sweeten with more tomato. Pass through a double sheet of wet muslin cloth.

For the taboulé

Bring the water, salt and oil to the boil. Add the couscous, stir and cover with cling film. Place on the side and leave for 3 minutes until the grains swell.

When tepid, add the seeds, pine kernels, raisins, herb julienne and finish by mixing in the olive oil, lemon juice and cayenne. Taste and correct the seasoning.

For the confit tomatoes

Blanch the tomatoes in boiling water for 5-10 seconds or until the skin starts to split, then refresh in iced water.

Peel the tomatoes and place in a bowl. Season with thyme, salt and sugar.

Place the tomatoes on a tray and place in oven at 80°C for 2 hours. At this point you will notice the tomatoes starting to dehydrate.

Remove tomatoes from oven, place in a container and reserve until needed.

To finish

Season the lamb with sea salt, sear in a hot pan with a small amount of rapeseed oil until light golden brown, place on a tray and put into a preheated oven at 200°C for about 6 minutes or until the core temperature is 55°C. Allow to rest for 6 minutes.

Warm the couscous, peas, broad beans and baby tomatoes and arrange nicely on the plate.

Warm the sauce, slice the lamb into thin slices and place onto the couscous.

Pour the sauce around the dish and finish with pea shoots.

The Oxford Kitchen
STRAWBERRY PANNA COTTA

This sumptuous summer treat brings traditional English strawberries and cream to a new level of pure deliciousness. The silkiness of panna cotta (literally meaning 'cooked cream' in Italian) marries perfectly with the bursting flavour of fresh strawberries. Serves 4

Ingredients

For the panna cotta:

15ml full fat milk

55ml double cream

200g strawberry purée

1 gelatine leaf (soaked in cold water)

115ml Greek yoghurt

30g caster sugar

For the strawberry gel:

200g frozen strawberries

20g icing sugar

Agar agar

For the strawberry muesli:

7g hazelnuts

7g flaked almonds

14g bran flakes

5g golden sultanas

5g freeze-dried strawberries (optional)

4ml vegetable oil

5g Demerara sugar

14g jumbo oats

11g honey

To serve:

Fresh strawberries

Basil cress

Strawberry sorbet or vanilla ice cream

Method

For the panna cotta

Warm milk and cream in a saucepan, then add the strawberry purée, sugar, gelatine and yoghurt.

Blend with a hand blender, pass through a fine sieve, pour into serving bowls and leave to set in the fridge for 1 hour.

For the strawberry gel

Combine the strawberries and sugar in a large bowl, place over a bain-marie and cook gently for about two hours.

Once the strawberries have released their juices, hang them in a muslin cloth overnight.

Weigh the strawberry juice. For every 100g of juice, add 1g of agar agar.

Place strawberry juice in a pan, add agar agar and bring to the boil, whisking continuously for 1 minute.

Pour onto a tray and leave to cool. Once cold, work with a hand blender until smooth.

For the strawberry muesli

Roast the hazelnuts and almonds at 170°C for 8-10 minutes, or until golden brown, then leave to cool.

Mix the bran flakes, sultanas and strawberries together and reserve.

Place the oil and sugar in a saucepan and heat gently until the sugar is dissolved.

Mix all the ingredients and leave to dry overnight on a tray.

To finish

Take the panna cotta out of the fridge and sprinkle with strawberry muesli.

Cut the strawberries into halves and place on the panna cotta with the basil cress.

Put drops of the strawberry gel over the top and finish with strawberry sorbet or vanilla ice cream.

The VILLAGE HUB

Pierreponts Café and Restaurant in Goring is perfectly situated to welcome the myriad walkers, cyclists and boaters that pass through the picturesque village, but it is their freshly made breakfasts, daily specials and friendly service that keeps loyal locals coming back time and time again.

From its beautiful spot near the river, the family-run Pierreponts Café wakes up the village with their homemade breakfasts, freshly baked breads from Birch Cottage Bakery and service with a smile. To give you that perfect kick-start to the day, a wide selection of food is on offer from their indulgent French toast with maple syrup, bananas and bacon, to simple egg and soldiers and fresh smoothies and juices.

The same care and attention goes into their lunches too, with dishes like avocado on toast with smoked salmon and a poached egg or their ever popular spinach pancake with chorizo, plus a whole host of specials that change depending on what produce is available locally. If it's not lunch you're after, there's always plenty on the bar to choose from, such as chilli and fennel sausage rolls, freshly made Scotch eggs, sweet and savoury tarts, amazing salads and a huge range of cakes and pastries.

Locality is key here; all of the ingredients are fresh and everything is sourced from as nearby as possible. All their meats come from the award-winning Vicars Game who only offer the highest quality produce. Fish is also brought in on a daily basis and when in season a local grower provides fruit and vegetables like baby chard, heritage tomatoes and beetroot's. In addition to this, local people often pop in to exchange a variety of great quality home grown produce for a coffee or breakfast.

This ethos extends further than the food they serve, as they offer space for local designers and makers to sell pottery, handmade jewellery and gift items. They even sell books by local authors. They also get involved in the village's many events, including the food festival, arts festival and providing flapjacks at the finish line of the Goring 10K.

Oozing charm and comfort, the décor at Pierreponts combines vintage wallpaper with mismatch furniture and cosy soft furnishings, including blankets for the outdoor area on those days that still have a slight chill in the air.

Whether you're popping by in the morning, visiting for a leisurely lunch or having a spot of dinner at their convivial Friday evenings, you'll be sure to get a warm welcome as well as some hearty food.

Pierreponts Café
BAKED LEMON SOLE, WITH BEETROOT AND PEA RISOTTO AND A PARMESAN CRISP

The delicate lemon soul works well with the earthiness of the beetroot and sugar sweet peas. Serves 4

Ingredients

1 shallot, chopped

½ stick celery, finely chopped

4 tbsp olive oil

200g risotto rice

350ml red wine

350ml vegetable stock

400g cooked peeled beetroot

8 fillets lemon sole

2 lemons, zest only

Salt and freshly ground black pepper

2 handfuls grated Parmesan

1 tsp fennel seeds

2 handfuls of peas

90ml double cream

Method

Preheat the oven to 180°C.

In a heated pan, sweat the shallot and celery in 2 tablespoons of the olive oil until translucent. Add the rice and stir well. Pour in the wine and the stock, turn the heat down, and simmer for around ten minutes, or until the rice is cooked but still on the firm side.

Meanwhile, purée the beetroot in a food processor until very smooth. Stir into the risotto. Season and cook for another ten minutes.

Flatten the lemon sole fillets on a tray, sprinkle with the lemon zest, salt, pepper and remaining olive oil. Roll them from tail to head and hold together with toothpicks. Place on some baking parchment, drizzle over a little olive oil and bake for ten minutes.

Separate one handful of the Parmesan into four circles on a piece of baking parchment. Sprinkle with the fennel seeds. Bake for about 8 minutes.

Add the peas, cream and remaining Parmesan to the risotto just before serving.

Serve the risotto in four bowls, placing the fillets of sole on top and finish with the Parmesan crisps.

Bon appetit!

Pure LUXURY

Every bar, individual chocolate or Easter egg from Plantation Chocolates is hand-made in Oxford. Each one is a labour of love, made with imagination and only the very finest natural ingredients.

Plantation Chocolates was founded by chocolate enthusiast Vivien Shelton in 2013. Vivien is always looking for the best quality and ethically sound ingredients. She uses the 70% chocolate made by award-winning Italian company Amedei; organic milk and white chocolate made by Original Beans; and UK producer Duffy's 83% chocolate from Ecuador and 100% from Panama.

To these Vivien adds delicious flavours and ingredients; green cardamom, rosemary and olive oil (handpicked by Vivien and her team in Italy), lemon and sea salt, fennel and candied orange plus many others. The staples of the range are the ever popular award-winning muscovado and sea salt caramel and the wonderful intense, dark praline (recipe below). She uses fresh cream, small amounts of local honey in all but the caramels, and very little else.

Vivien's artisan hand-crafted confections are made in small batches and packaged with the same level of attention to detail in luxurious gift boxes tied beautifully with ribbon. The stunning range has won over fine food lovers in Oxford. A perfect gift for any chocolate lover.

Plantation Chocolates
NUT PRALINE

Many people, including me, find most nut pralines too sweet. My recipe is for those who like their chocolate intense! Makes 80

Ingredients

150g hazelnuts

150g almonds

225g unrefined caster sugar

100g 80% chocolate, broken into pieces

100g 100% chocolate, broken into pieces

Tempered chocolate, for dipping (optional)

Cocoa powder, for rolling (optional)

Method

Preheat the oven 180°C.

Roast the nuts in moderate oven until lightly browned and then remove the skins. Heat the sugar in a heavy pan until it caramelises. Pour in the warm, roasted nuts and stir quickly to coat in the caramel. Pour onto a baking sheet and leave to cool. Break roughly and put into a food processor or grinder. Blend until you have a fairly smooth paste.

You will need 420g of the nut paste. Place the weighed-out nut paste with the chocolate pieces in a heatproof bowl and set over a bain-marie to melt. Temper this mix by taking it to 48°C, then sit the bowl in cold water and continue stirring until it reaches 29°C, then gently bring back to 32.5°C. Make sure no moisture gets into the praline mixture.

Either pipe this mixture into chocolate-lined moulds, or leave to cool then roll into balls as you would truffles. Either dip in more tempered chocolate (tempering it as described above) or roll in cocoa powder.

Field TO FORK

A pub, restaurant, farm and butchers... The Pointer in Brill is a shining example of farm to fork dining at its very best.

When James Rogers bought The Pointer in 2011, he had an ambitious vision to bring the historic red-brick pub back to being a real village hub with top-notch food and community spirit at its heart. Records show that ale was first sold on the premises in the 16th century and James has been uncovering its fascinating past as he has restored the ancient walls and beautiful stonework back to their former glory.

Today the pub is the heart and soul of the community again, welcoming regulars day after day who come to enjoy a drink in the pub or a locally sourced meal at the award-winning restaurant. And when they say "locally sourced", at The Pointer they mean just that. With their own farm currently producing about 70% of the ingredients they use in the restaurant, this is a team who don't do things by halves. In the summer they have been known to serve incredible seasonal dishes with more than 15 ingredients – every single one of which was grown or reared on their own farm.

The 240-acre farm, just a couple of miles down the road, produces everything from garlic, onions and potatoes to unusual crops like pencil aubergines and fresh fruits such as apples and grapes, which are then pressed into fruit juices and served in the bar. Longhorn cattle graze on the lush pastures, Tamworth pigs are slow-reared happily, lambs roam freely and ducks, chickens and guinea fowl enjoy the highest free-range welfare standards.

Such commitment to ethical and sustainable farming also ensures the best tasting produce, of course – something exhibited by the on-site butchers, whose passion for the excellent rare-breed meat is evident in their knowledge and enthusiasm for the produce.

It's on display in the meals prepared in the restaurant too, where countless awards are testament to the incredible quality that is achieved when ingredients are grown, prepared and cooked with such care and attention to detail. With two AA rosettes under their belt and praise from critics across the country, this family-friendly pub has managed to combine village comfort with remarkable cooking.

The Pointer

cer and beef have made us what we

The Pointer's
VEAL PIE

The Pointer buy all their veal from Norton's Farm. Owner Lucy Ashby breeds a small number of Jersey cows and produces some of the finest veal in the country. Here it is, our recipe for English rose veal pie in puff pastry.
Serves 4

Ingredients

1kg veal shin on the bone

250g veal sweet breads, peeled and blended

1 litre beef stock

500ml white wine

4 carrots, peeled and chopped

1 onion, peeled and chopped

2 bay leaves

1 tbsp chopped thyme

4 cloves garlic

100g picked and washed baby spinach leaves

2 tbsp Dijon mustard

4 sheets all-butter puff pastry sheets (30cm x 20cm)

2 egg yolks, for glazing

Method

Preheat the oven to 160°C.

Seal the veal shin in a casserole pot. Add the sweetbreads, beef stock, white wine, vegetables, herbs and garlic. Braise in the oven for 2 hours 30 minutes on a low heat.

Remove the meat from the casserole and pick off the meat from the bone. Pass the stock through a fine sieve and let it reduce on the stove until it thickens to a syrup.

Cook the spinach in a pan, drain and add to the meat. Add the mustard. Slowly add the sauce until the meat is just moist – too much and the pastry will go soggy. Roll into four 250g balls. Cut each sheet of puff pastry into a 10 x 10cm square and 20 x 20cm square for the top. Place the meat on the bottom sheet, carefully place the larger sheet on top and seal the edges by pressing together. Let them set in the fridge for about 1 hours 30 minutes.

Preheat the oven to 200°C.

Egg wash each pie and bake straight from the fridge in the hot oven for about 20 minutes until golden brown. Take them out and leave to rest for 5-10 minutes. Serve with vegetables, potatoes or even a light summer salad.

The Pointer's
BLOOD ORANGE POSSET

A stunning recipe when blood oranges are in season.
Serves 12

Ingredients

For the base posset:

600ml milk

800g double cream

5 blood oranges

300g caster sugar

5 gelatine leaves (soaked in cold water)

For the blood orange jelly:

300g blood orange juice

50g caster sugar

2 gelatine leaves (soaked in cold water)

For the second posset layer:

400g double cream

50g lemon juice

50g blood orange juice

40g caster sugar

For the amaretto jelly:

250ml amaretto

2 gelatine leaves (soaked in cold water)

For the blood orange sorbet:

1kg freshly squeezed blood orange juice

250g water

250g caster sugar

75g liquid glucose

To garnish:

Blood orange segments, candied orange slices or crushed almond biscuits

Method

For the base posset, simmer the milk, cream and the zest and juice of four blood oranges, then let it cool to infuse the flavour. Add the sugar, soaked gelatine leaves and the zest and juice of the fifth blood orange and pass through a sieve. Divide into glasses and leave to set.

For the blood orange jelly, bring the blood orange juice and sugar to the boil, add the soaked gelatine leaves and allow to cool. When cool, pour a thin layer of jelly over the base posset.

For the second posset layer, bring all the ingredients to the boil. Let it cool down and set on top of jelly layer.

For the amaretto jelly, gently heat the amaretto and add the gelatine, but do not boil. Pour into a separate container and allow to set.

For the blood orange sorbet, bring all the ingredients to the boil and freeze in an ice cream maker.

Once you have all the above components made, serve the posset with a ball of the blood orange sorbet and small pieces of the amaretto jelly. You can then garnish with fresh segments of blood orange, candied orange slices and even crush some almond biscuits on top for added texture.

A Quince-essential CAFÉ

Situated on the banks of the Thames in Henley, The Quince Tree café at the River and Rowing Museum champions the best of British, whilst supporting local suppliers.

A key part of The Quince Tree ethos is to source high quality products from local reliable suppliers to make simple, fresh and delicious dishes. All of the meat is British where possible, the eggs are free-range, the fish is sustainably sourced and the specials board regularly features dishes based around seasonal ingredients. From pastries and breakfast to salads and signature Sunday roasts, there's plenty to enjoy in the café. Sweet items in the delicatessen counter, offering a delicious range of homemade cakes and sweet treats, are available to eat in or take away.

Picnic hampers are also offered during the summer for those who wish to enjoy a peaceful day in the sunshine aboard a boat or on the meadows overlooking the river. Including signature favourites like freshly made 'scrumpy' cider sausage rolls, Scotch eggs, salads, sandwiches and chocolate brownies, they're all presented in a hamper ready to pick up on the day of your trip.

The bright and bustling café boasts a stunning outdoor terrace, as does The River & Rowing Museum's private Thames Room, which is the perfect space for groups for up to 180 people offering views of the river and picturesque Oxfordshire countryside. Whether a business lunch, conference, dinner party or wedding, The Quince Tree team are on hand to help you host your event.

Their second venue is at Clifton Nurseries; London's oldest garden emporium and one of the most tranquil spots in the city. Enjoy the perfect day out in one of London's hidden treasures with a delicious brunch or relaxed lunch set in a beautiful glasshouse amongst the stunning flowers and plants.

At either venue you'll be guaranteed food that is quintessentially British, with dishes that have been created with the local community in mind; from farmers and cheese makers to butchers and bakers, each dish combines the best of the region's culinary offerings.

The Quince Tree
SCRUMPER'S SCOTCH EGG

Makes 8 eggs

Ingredients

8 free-range eggs (soft boiled for 6 minutes then cooled in cold water)

1 litre vegetable oil, for frying

For the sausage meat:

½ tsp English mustard powder

1 pinch smoked paprika

1 Bramley apple, peeled and finely diced

1 tsp parsley, finely chopped

1 tsp chives, finely chopped

1 pinch table salt

800g sausage meat

For the pane (breadcrumbs):

200g plain flour

Salt and pepper

2 Cotswold brown eggs

10ml semi-skimmed milk

100g panko breadcrumbs

20g finely grated pecorino cheese

To serve:

Piccalilli

Brown sauce

Method

For the sausage meat

Add all of the spices, diced apple, herbs and salt to the sausage meat and mix well. Take care not to over work the meat as this will begin to toughen it up.

Divide the mixture into 8 balls.

To assemble

Prepare your working area by getting a little pot of water ready for your hands. Place the bowl of sausage meat on the left, then the cooled eggs, and then lastly a cling film lined tray.

Wet your hands so the sausage doesn't stick. Flatten the ball out in the palm of your hand, roughly the size of a large coaster.

Carefully wrap one ball of sausage meat around the first egg, trying to make sure it is even and all the air is removed.

Place the first wrapped egg on the cling film lined tray. Repeat the process for the next seven eggs.

Have a quick tidy up and set yourself three new bowls. In the first one place the flour seasoned with salt and pepper. In the second lightly beat the egg together with the milk. In the third mix together the panko breadcrumbs and pecorino.

Dust the egg in flour, dip it in the beaten egg and finally roll in the breadcrumbs. Try to keep one hand for the wet mix and one hand for the dry or you will end up with well breaded fingers!

Heat the oil to a moderate heat and then deep fry your Scotch eggs until golden brown.

We like to finish the eggs in the oven for a really crunchy casing and find that 160-165°C is good for this.

Season immediately and leave to cool a little. Enjoy warm with some piccalilli or brown sauce.

The Quince Tree
MUSHROOM TORTELLINI

Rich and delicious. Serves 6

Ingredients

For the pasta:
200g semolina flour
100g 00 flour
2 free-range egg yolks
2 free-range eggs
For ricotta filling:
150g ricotta
Salt, to taste
Nutmeg, to taste
50ml extra virgin olive oil
100g spinach, steamed and chopped
75g Parmesan, ideally aged 36 months
For the butternut squash purée:
1 butternut squash, cut into rough
chunks
1 garlic clove, thinly sliced
Sprig of thyme
50ml olive oil
10g butter
Salt and pepper, to taste
50ml double cream
20g cold butter, diced
For the herb oil:
500g olive oil
2 good pinches of cracked black pepper
Sprig of rosemary
180g garlic, cut in half
300g parsley
300g spinach
For the duxelle mix:
200g Paris mushrooms
200g pied de mouton (hedgehog
mushrooms)
200g pied bleu (wood blewit
mushrooms)
2 banana shallots
2 cloves garlic
¼ bunch thyme
100ml dry white wine
⅓ bunch parsley
For the sauté mushrooms:
50g ceps
50g girolles
50g pied de mouton (hedgehog
mushrooms)
50g pied bleus (wood blewit
mushrooms)
50g black trompettes
To serve:
Micro herbs
Fresh Parmesan

Method

For the pasta

In a mixing bowl, mix the two flours and make a well in the centre. Add the egg yolks, whole eggs and a pinch of salt. Mix all of the ingredients together until you obtain a consistent dough.

Knead vigorously for at least 15 minutes then wrap the dough with cling film. Leave to rest in the fridge for at least 2 hours.

For the tortellini filling

To make the filling, whisk the ricotta in a medium sized bowl, add a little salt, grated nutmeg and a drizzle of extra virgin olive oil. Add the chopped steamed spinach and a generous handful of Parmesan. Transfer the filling to a piping bag.

To make the tortellini, cut the rested dough in half. Roll out the dough in a pasta machine or with a good rolling pin, keeping the other half covered.

Use an 8cm pastry cutter to cut out circles of the pasta. Keep the pasta you are not using covered by a tea towel.

To form the tortellini, place a teaspoon of your filling in the centre of a circle and moisten the edge with a very small amount of water using a pastry brush.

Gently fold the pasta over and seal at the top. Work your fingers down the edges to seal, pushing out any air bubbles as you go. Repeat until you have used all the pasta and filling, storing them on a floured tray until you are ready to cook them.

For the butternut squash purée

Preheat the oven to 170°C.

Place the butternut squash onto a large roasting tray with the garlic, sprig of thyme, olive oil, butter, season to taste with salt and pepper. Place the tray into the oven and roast for 40-45 minutes, or until the squash flesh is very tender. Remove from the oven and scoop out the flesh with a spoon. Place the cooked butternut squash into a blender and purée with the double cream until very smooth. Add the 20g butter and blend again until all of the butter is incorporated. This will give the purée a beautiful glossy finish. Adjust the seasoning.

If making the purée in advance, don't add the butter until ready to serve. Chill the purée and store in the fridge. Reheat when ready to serve and add the butter at the last minute.

For the herb oil

Add the olive oil, black pepper, rosemary and garlic to a pan and bring to the boil.

Remove from the stove, cover and reserve. After 1 hour, filter the mix and reserve the oily sauce.

In another pan, blanch the parsley and spinach. Cool them down in ice water, remove and leave to dry. Finally, mix the spinach, parsley and the oily sauce in a blender.

For the duxelle

Clean and dry all of the mushrooms and chop as finely as possible.

Mince the shallots, garlic and thyme and sweat them together in a pan.

Add the mushrooms and sauté gently until all the moisture from the mushrooms has evaporated. Pour over the white wine and cook for about 10 more minutes until it has been absorbed. Add the fresh chopped parsley and salt and pepper to season.

For the sauté mushrooms

Clean and dry the mushrooms then cut into large pieces.

Roast them in a hot pan with olive oil, garlic and thyme.

To serve

Blanch the tortellini in plenty of hot salted water until they start to float.

Whilst they are cooking dress the warm mushroom duxelle on a plate in a square or circle shape using a setting ring.

Place five tortellini around the duxelle.

Spoon over the sauté mushrooms and dress with the micro herbs.

Dot around the herb oil and finish with a good grating of fresh Parmesan.

The Quince Tree

KEDGEREE

Serves 5-6 as a light lunch

Ingredients

For the haddock:

¼ Spanish onion

4 cloves

250g natural smoked haddock

1.25 litres full fat milk

3 bay leaves

Handful of parsley

½ unwaxed lemon, zest

For the rice:

430g basmati rice

50g butter

200g Spanish onions, finely diced

7g mild curry powder

10g green cardamom

625ml fresh or good quality shop bought chicken or vegetable stock

100g peas

Chopped parsley

Some poaching liquor from the haddock

To serve:

6 poached eggs

Finely sliced red chilli, seeds removed if you prefer less heat

Coriander cress

Method

For the poached eggs

Prepare these in advance by placing the cooked eggs in iced water. You can then heat them through in simmering water for a few minutes just before serving.

For the haddock

Stud the onion with the cloves. Add all of the haddock ingredients to a saucepan and simmer until the fish is just cooked (about 8 minutes). Remove from the heat.

Carefully remove the fish. Leave the milk mixture to infuse until it has completely cooled.

Skin and gently flake the fish, checking for any residual bones.

Reserve for later.

For the rice

To remove the starch, wash the rice until the water runs clear.

Melt the butter in a large pan and add in the diced onion, sweating them down until translucent. Add the freshly ground spices and cook out for a few minutes to take away the rawness.

Add in the basmati rice and allow it to roast in the butter for a few minutes. The rice will absorb most of the butter in the pan.

As with making a risotto, begin by adding in three-quarters of the hot vegetable stock. The rice will absorb the liquor so continue adding the stock until the rice is cooked al dente.

Add the peas and parsley followed by a spoonful of the haddock liquor. Finish by gently folding in the flaked haddock, being careful not to mash it into the rice.

Spoon out the kedgeree into warm bowls and top with the poached eggs, chillies and the coriander cress.

The Quince Tree

CARPACCIO OF VENISON, PARMESAN EMULSION

Serves 12 as a starter

Ingredients

For the carpaccio:

430g trimmed venison loin

5 juniper berries

1 sprig of thyme

1 sprig of rosemary

1 tsp Maldon sea salt

20ml rapeseed oil

5 grinds of freshly milled black pepper

For the salt-baked beets:

1 bunch baby candy beets

80g Maldon sea salt

For the Parmesan emulsion:

3 egg yolks

60g Parmesan, finely grated

2 tsp garlic, finely grated

1 tsp fish sauce

1 tsp Dijon mustard

Pinch cracked black pepper

Pinch of salt

250ml oil (mix 125ml of pomace oil and 125ml of light rapeseed oil)

50ml water

For the vinaigrette:

1 tsp Dijon mustard

150ml rapeseed oil

150ml vegetable oil

1 lemon

Salt and pepper, to taste

50ml water

Pinch cayenne pepper

For the garnish (handful of each per person):

Rocket

Sliced radish

Shaved Parmesan

Shallot slivers

Method

For the carpaccio

Trim the venison of all the silver skin, fat and any sinews. There shouldn't be too much trim as it is very lean meat but, if you prefer to, ask your butcher to help when ordering. Lightly oil the meat and in a searing hot pan seal on all sides. Make sure the extraction is on as this part can be rather smoky! Rolling it around the pan with a good pair of tongs is best as it will spit a little. You only need a very light sear - just about 1mm on the outside of the meat. Finally sear both ends.

Whilst the venison cools, place the remaining ingredients in a pestle and mortar and crush well.

Layer several pieces of suitably sized cling film to roll the venison, four is usually sufficient. Rub the venison with the herb salt ensuring an even coating then roll it in the cling film on a table away from you, making it in to a very tight sausage shape – hold the ends of the cling film to tighten it up, then tie up the ends and place in the freezer for at least 3 hours. Once you are happy that it is rolled into a good sausage shape and as tight as you can get it, tie off the ends and place in the freezer for at least 3 hours. This can even be done the day before.

Once chilled or frozen, the venison is ready to slice and you can remove the cling film. Slice the desired amount of meat and then lay the carpaccio onto cling film, reserving in the fridge until you're ready to serve.

For the salt-baked beets

Sprinkle a sheet of parchment paper with sea salt.

Trim the stalks and roots from the beetroot's, place onto the salt and cook in a preheated moderate oven for 40 minutes or until just cooked.

After allowing the beetroot to cool, peel using a small knife and reserve, ready for later, in the fridge.

For the Parmesan emulsion

Blend the egg yolks, Parmesan, garlic, fish sauce, Dijon mustard, salt and pepper in a food processor until well combined. With the motor running slowly pour in the oils until the mixture becomes thick and silky.

Adjust the consistency with the water until it just coats the back of a spoon. Store for later.

For the vinaigrette

Place all the ingredients in a squeezy bottle or mason jar and shake vigorously until combined. Check the seasoning and store in the fridge until needed. Shake to bring it back together when ready to serve.

To serve

Lay five pieces of carpaccio on a plate. Dot around some drops of the Parmesan emulsion, add a few quartered pieces of the candy beets, thinly sliced radish, shallots, a little of each of the herbs and the shaved Parmesan.

Finally scatter on some sea salt and a little drizzle of the lemon vinaigrette.

The Quince Tree
MACARONS

A French classic. Makes 35

Ingredients

For the macarons:

160g ground almonds

170g icing sugar

120ml egg whites from about 4 medium free-range eggs, separated into 2 equal batches

160g caster sugar

50ml water

Powdered red colouring

For the ganache filling:

110g dark chocolate, finely chopped

120ml double cream

50ml lime juice (approximately three limes)

25g unsalted butter, room temperature

For the raspberry coulis:

300g fresh raspberries

50g sugar

Squeeze of lemon juice

2 x 8g sachets pectin

Method

For the macarons

Place the ground almonds, icing sugar and one half (110g) of the egg whites in a mixing bowl and mix to form a smooth paste. Set aside.

Place the remaining egg whites in a clean mixing bowl and begin to whisk. If you are using an electric whisk, make sure it is on a low speed.

Place the caster sugar and water into a pan and heat gently to dissolve the sugar. Once dissolved, increase the heat and use a sugar thermometer to monitor the temperature. When the temperature of the sugar syrup reaches 105°C, start to beat the egg whites, on high speed if you're using an electric whisk. Once the syrup is at 118°C pour it slowly down the side of the mixer bowl, avoiding the moving whisk. Continue to whisk on high until the mixture has cooled slightly and you have a shiny peaked meringue mixture – the bowl should no longer be hot to the touch, but still warm. Add the colouring and whisk to combine.

Fold one third of the meringue into the almond mixture with a spatula and mix carefully until incorporated. Repeat with another third of the mixture and when incorporated, fold in the remaining meringue and mix until smooth and shiny.

Transfer the mixture into a piping bag fitted with a plain 10mm nozzle and pipe 45mm (the size of a 2 pence piece) rounds on to baking trays lined with silicone sheets or baking paper.

Leave to rest at room temperature for 30 minutes so that a slight skin forms on the top of the macarons.

While the macarons are resting, preheat the oven to 130°C. Place the baking trays in the oven for 14 minutes until the macarons just peel off the paper. Allow to cool down completely before filling and decorating.

For the ganache filling

Gently melt the chocolate and cream together in a bowl set on top of a pan of simmering water. Add the lime juice gradually to the mixture. Then gradually add the butter and incorporate fully. Remove from the heat, cover and chill in the fridge.

For the raspberry coulis

Push the raspberries through a sieve and collect the juice in a small pan. Add the sugar and lemon juice and bring the mixture up to the boil. Once boiling, add the pectin and whisk for 2-3 minutes. Remove from the heat and leave to cool.

Transfer the ganache to a piping bag and assemble the macarons. Pipe the ganache in the middle, top with raspberry 'coulis' and sandwich with the other half of the macaron.

Store in an airtight container or carefully in a zip lock bag for a maximum of 4 days. Unfilled macaron cookies can successfully be frozen for a month. Allow the cookies to come to room temperature before filling.

Catering the
COTSWOLDS

A small multi award-winning fine food company based in Chipping Norton in the magnificent Oxfordshire Cotswolds, Ross & Ross Food offers unrivalled wedding and event catering and inspired handmade food gifts.

Set up in 2011 by Ross Bearman and Ross Whitmill (they offer no prizes for guessing how they came up with the business name!), Ross & Ross Food has grown and developed into an award-winning fine food company, supporting local Cotswolds producers along their journey and championing the best of British food.

Having both worked in the fine food industry for over 15 years, Ross and Ross shared an enthusiasm for top-quality ingredients, a love of local Cotswolds produce and a special interest in British charcuterie. Ross & Ross Food began life with a range of pâté's and terrine's for high-end stockists like Harrods and Daylesford Organic, as well as small farm shops.

Five years later and the business has expanded into two main areas – event and wedding catering on one side and handmade British food gifts on the other.

They have made their mark on the local food scene by catering many different types of event, from local weddings and parties to clients such as Prime Minister David Cameron and the British Cheese Awards. No matter what the occasion, their signature style is one of no fuss, high quality and beautiful presentation. Using the very best local and seasonal ingredients goes without saying, of course.

Their friendly demeanour and relaxed, informal approach paired with their efficient professionalism has proved a successful combination, with clients always reporting just how at ease they were made to feel – "like working with a particularly efficient old friend", according to one satisfied customer.

Their small team of five also find time to run monthly pop-up restaurants at local venues. These events usually sell out fast, but for those lucky guests who attend, they are in for a five-course feast of creative cooking celebrating the bounty of the Oxfordshire Cotswolds.

Their inspired range of gift boxes includes the award-winning homemade curing kit, which contains everything you need to cure your own bacon at home – just add the pork! They have also created a range of 'man boxes' containing craft beer or cider paired with artisan British charcuterie, chutney and triple-cooked crackling. What's not to love about that?

Ross & Ross Food

Ross & Ross Food

Event & Wedding Caterers
~
Handmade British Food Gifts

T: 01608 645 503   E: events@rossandrossfood.co.uk

www.rossandrossfood.co.uk

Ross & Ross Food

SLOW-ROASTED SHOULDER OF ENGLISH LAMB, BOULANGÈRE POTATOES AND SALSA VERDE

This is a lovely recipe to make when English lamb is in season.
You can make the onion jam and salsa verde in advance. Serves 6

Ingredients

Shoulder of English lamb (bone-in and rolled), approx. 2 kg

1 clove garlic, sliced

8 large waxy potatoes, peeled and very thinly sliced (use a mandoline or sharp knife)

½ bunch thyme leaves, stalks removed and chopped

50g melted butter

1 recipe of onion jam (see below)

700ml chicken stock

Salt and pepper to taste

Salsa verde, to serve (see below)

For the onion jam:

45ml English rapeseed oil

3 large white onions, finely sliced

1 bay leaf

Salt and pepper to taste

For the salsa verde:

30g flat leaf parsley, finely chopped

15g fresh mint, picked and finely chopped

20g banana shallots, peeled and finely chopped

20g gherkins, drained and finely chopped

20g capers (in brine), drained and finely chopped

100ml English rapeseed oil

30ml sunflower oil

15ml lemon juice

Method

For the onion jam, heat the oil in a large pan, add the onions, bay leaf and salt. Gently cook on a low heat for about 45-60 minutes until soft and turning golden brown. Season with salt and pepper. If you are not using it immediately for the roasted lamb and boulangère potatoes, sterilise a glass jar and lid then add the hot jam. Seal and store in a cool dark place until needed.

For the salsa verde, mix all the ingredients together and season to taste. Store in the fridge until needed. This can be made a few days in advance. Remove an hour before ready to serve.

For the roasted lamb and boulangère potatoes, preheat the oven to 130°C/250°F/Gas Mark ½. Using a sharp knife, pierce the skin of the lamb around five times and push in the garlic slices and season all over. Set aside.

Mix the sliced potatoes, thyme, melted butter and onion jam together and season. Layer the potato mix in a deep roasting tray and pour over the chicken stock. Put the lamb on top of the potatoes and roast in the oven for 4-5 hours until the lamb is tender and the potatoes are cooked through. Remove from the oven, cover in tin foil and leave to rest for 20 minutes.

Once rested, the lamb bone should simply pull out, then carve in slices or use two forks to pull apart. Serve with buttered cavolo nero and the salsa verde.

Doubly DELICIOUS

Recently re-launched Sudbury House Hotel is proud to have been awarded four AA Silver Stars and three AA Rosettes for their impressive restaurants.

Nestling on the edge of the Cotswolds between Oxford and Swindon in Faringdon, the Sudbury House Hotel and their two restaurants, the Magnolia Brasserie and Restaurant 56, received two awards in 2015, just months after a complete refurbishment was finished. Sudbury House and Magnolia Brasserie was presented with the new AA Four Star Silver Award for the whole 'guest and diner' experience, whilst Andrew Scott from the hotel's fine-dining establishment Restaurant 56 was awarded with 3 AA Rosettes.

Such accolades are pretty impressive, as it is just under two years since the hotel and restaurant started a complete refurbishment, during which time the hotel remained open. Driven by a clear vision, the passionate team from Sudbury House are extremely proud of the results of their hard work and are striving for even higher future awards.

Ben Bullen is head chef of the new Magnolia Brasserie, which offers contemporary dining with a feature kitchen and wood-burning stove. This creates an exciting theatre for diners to watch, as talented chef's work in front of them. Having previously worked with Andrew Scott, Ben was keen to be part of the team and, after only a few months, he is already creating outstanding food.

Andrew Scott, who joined Restaurant 56 as head chef in January 2014 from The Curlew in East Sussex, is putting Sudbury House on the culinary map thanks to his British food using classic combinations with a contemporary edge. Together with his sous chef Nick Bennett (fresh from the MasterChef – The Professionals final) and restaurant manager Sergio Martinez Rios, Andrew and his team have quickly established a restaurant with a reputation for excellence.

Once owned by Sir William Glock, the BBC controller of music, the property was purchased in May 2013 by an independent business man who immediately started transforming the building through sensitive refurbishment, creating a luxurious 49-bedroom hotel with the fine-dining Restaurant 56 located in the "old house". Now restored and decorated with a classic style, infusing modern design with carefully selected antiques, artworks, luxurious fabrics and soft furnishings, both the hotel and restaurant facilities offer guests and diners a truly enhanced visitor experience.

The main part of Sudbury House features a more contemporary design. Guests can enjoy a warm, friendly bar and lounge whilst bedrooms are spacious and well-appointed, offering everything you could need. With plans underway for new floral additions outside and extended kitchen gardens, the existing al-fresco dining facilities and relaxing outdoor spaces are set to be made even more beautiful.

Sudbury House

Magnolia Brasserie

IBERICO PORK CHOP, CHORIZO AND BUTTERBEAN, DILL AND MINT GREMOLATA

When it comes to cooking I like to use clean flavours and simple cooking methods, this recipe isn't a twist or a spin on anything less than beautiful ingredients and explosions of flavour.
I hope you enjoy this recipe as much as I do. Chorizo is definitely one of my favourite ingredients and together with the Iberico pork chop it's a perfect marriage.
Recipe by Ben Bullen. Serves 4

Ingredients

4 Iberico pork chops

500g dried butterbeans, soaked in cold water for 24 hours

A few large chunks of onion, carrot and celery, for cooking the beans

Bouquet garni (optional)

1 onion, diced

2 sticks celery, diced

2 carrots, diced

1 chilli, deseeded and finely chopped

2 cloves garlic, finely chopped

2 tsp smoked paprika

250g chorizo, diced

200ml red wine (Rioja would be my suggestion)

1 tin of chopped tomatoes

Chopped parsley, to finish

For the gremolata:

½ bunch dill

½ bunch parsley

½ bunch mint

2 cloves garlic

1 lemon

200ml olive oil

100ml vegetable oil

50g capers

Salt and pepper to taste

Method

The pork chops will not need much preparation. You can trim off a little of the fat from around the edge, but to me, this holds a lot of flavour.

Drain the soaked butterbeans and place in a pan. Cover with fresh cold water and simmer with some large chunks of onion, carrot and celery. You can add a bouquet garni to this if you wish. Let the beans cook and become tender on a low simmer, drain when cooked and leave to cool.

Heat a medium sized heavy based pan, sweat down the onion, carrot, celery and chilli without colouring, then add the garlic to the vegetables. Add the smoked paprika and diced chorizo, and let the fats start to come out of the chorizo as this will enhance that smoky chorizo flavour.

Deglaze with red wine and let the alcohol cook out. Next add the chopped tomatoes and a little water (you can use chicken stock if you so wish).

Let the ragout simmer for 30-40 minutes until all the flavours have married together, then add the butterbeans and adjust the seasoning.

For the gremolata

You will need to finely chop all the herbs, chop the garlic as finely as possible and zest the lemon finely. Next mix in the oils and capers, squeeze in the lemon juice and season to your own taste.

Cook the pork chops by either grilling on both sides for 4 minutes each or, in a heavy-based ovenproof frying pan, heat a little oil (you won't need much as the chop will render down the fat and create a gorgeous caramelisation), seal the pork chops on both sides and put in the oven for about 4 minutes. Let the pork chops rest while you bring the butterbeans back up to a simmer and finish with chopped parsley.

Serve the chop on top of the beans and add a generous helping of the gremolata. Serve with some nice purple sprouting broccoli.

Restaurant 56

CHERRY CHEESECAKE CANNELLONI, FLAPJACK, PISTACHIO CURD

When Nick and I create new recipes and dish ideas we often think and brainstorm about what we liked to eat when we were growing up... We both hope you enjoy making our spin on the traditional cheesecake. By Andrew Scott and Nick Bennett. Serves 8

Ingredients

For the jelly:

200g cherry purée

100ml water

50g sugar

3g agar agar

3 gelatine leaves

For the cheesecake:

200g white chocolate

200g cream cheese

1 vanilla pod

1 gelatine sheet

320ml double cream

For the flapjack:

5 tbsp honey

50g butter

50g sugar

100g porridge oats

For the pistachio curd:

6 eggs

3 yolks

125g butter

150g sugar

2 tbsp pistachio paste

For the cherry sorbet:

500ml cherry purée

250ml water

230g sugar

20ml liquid glucose

For the poached cherries:

250g pitted cherries cut neatly in half

250ml Port

250ml red wine

300g caster sugar

For the cherry gel:

250ml cherry purée

200ml stock syrup

50ml water

5g agar agar

To garnish:

50g pistachios, pulsed

Method

For the jelly

Soak the gelatine in cold water. Boil the purée, water and sugar. When boiling, whisk in the agar agar. Ensure you reboil the mixture. Squeeze off the gelatine leaves and add to the mix. Pour into a glass bowl. Allow to cool slightly for 3 minutes. Spray a tray with grease spray, place acetate on top and ladle the mix onto the acetate, then spread to form an even layer. Place in the fridge for at least 20 minutes.

For the cheesecake

Soak the gelatine in cold water. Melt the white chocolate in a glass bowl over simmering water. Warm the cream cheese and vanilla pod in a small saucepan. When simmering, add the gelatine to the mix. Then add the cream cheese mix into the chocolate. Lightly whip the cream to form soft peaks. When the chocolate mix has cooled slightly, fold the cream into the mix. Pipe the mix into tubes and set into the fridge.

For the pistachio curd

Place the eggs, yolks and sugar into a pan and cook at 100°C for 5 minutes stirring continuously, then blend. Alternatively you can use a Thermomix if you have one. Add the butter and nut paste, then mix all together. Pour the mix into a piping bag and store in the fridge until needed.

For the flapjack

In a small saucepan, mix the honey, butter and sugar together. Bring the mixture to the boil. Remove from the heat and add the oats. Mix it all together. Bake in the oven at 160°C for 10-12 minutes. Leave to cool on a wire rack.

For the sorbet

Mix all the ingredients together in a saucepan and gently heat to dissolve the sugar. Once dissolved, cool down then churn in an ice cream machine.

For the cherries

Bring the Port, wine and sugar to a light simmer. Place the cherries in the pan and remove from the heat. Cover in cling film and leave to cool down at room temperature.

For the fluid gel

Boil the purée, water and stock syrup. Add the agar agar and re-boil. Refrigerate until set, then blitz back to a smooth gel. Transfer to a squeezy bottle.

To assemble the cheesecake

Remove one of the cheesecakes from the tube. Place horizontally on the jelly sheet and score a knife on the jelly sheet, either end of the cheesecake. Wrap the jelly around the cheesecake and cut into three. Plate up as the picture.

The art of the
CHOCOLATIER

At Tutu Delicious, on Watlington's thriving high street, every artisan chocolate is hand-crafted on the premises by talented, passionate and creative chocolatier Zoe Haynes.

The aroma, the glossy shine and the irresistible mouth-feel… chocolate has the ability to awaken all our senses. For Zoe Haynes, chocolate has become a way of life. Zoe studied art before embarking on a career in food, having worked for renowned artist Richard Hamiliton and then as a chef under Richard Neat at the Michelin-starred Pied a Terre – it was here that her interest in the artistry of chocolate really took hold, bringing her two passions together.

Zoe began making chocolate for family and friends and it didn't take long for everyone who tasted them to realise that she had real talent. In December 2011, Zoe's home town of Watlington welcomed her shop, Tutu Delicious, to its high street. Enthusiasm, commitment and unwavering family support were the foundation of Tutu Delicious, and today, these principles remain at the heart of the family-led business, which she now runs with her sister Liza.

The business began to flourish thanks to word-of-mouth recommendations and praise on social media, and Zoe soon found it wasn't just the discerning locals that were popping in to buy her goodies, but chocolate-lovers from far and wide who were seeking out artisan confections of superior quality.

Everything is hand-crafted at Tutu Delicious – you can pop into the workshop and watch Zoe shaping, cutting and dipping her chocolates. In the early days, she simply had a glass screen separating her work space from the shop area. Being immersed in the whole experience won over all those who visited the shop – not only having beautiful truffles to look at, they were surrounded by the intense aroma and could ask Zoe all about the ingredients, techniques and flavours. Today, Tutu Delicious has expanded into the adjacent premises, but retains the workshop next door for customers to pop in.

At Tutu Delicious, it's all about sharing passion and enthusiasm with customers – whether it's the excitement of sourcing incredible local ingredients or developing distinct new flavours, Zoe adores the creative process and sharing her love of quality and experimentation. She bubbles over with enthusiasm as soon as she gets talking about chocolate, and her passion is clearly contagious, with customers returning time and time again to see what exciting new treats she has made or to stock up on those irresistible classics.

Zoe's skill and attention to detail was awarded with recognition for various products at The Great Taste Awards, with the coveted three stars being awarded to her apricot and rosemary chocolates. With demand continually increasing, an apprentice chocolatier now working under Zoe's wing and a close-knit team of staff in the shop, the future certainly looks sweet for Zoe and Liza.

Tutu Delicious Chocolate
RASPBERRY TRUFFLES

These truffles are simple to make at home but make very impressive gifts for lucky family members and friends. Use the very best milk chocolate you can find to ensure delicious results. Makes 30

Ingredients

300g good-quality milk chocolate

65ml double cream

15ml glucose syrup

65ml raspberry purée (fresh raspberries, puréed, sieved and pips removed)

15ml Framboise (optional)

Raspberry powder, for dusting

Method

Break the chocolate into pieces and place in a heatproof glass bowl. Melt over a pan of gently simmering water, ensuring no water gets into the chocolate. Once it has melted, take the bowl off the pan and set aside.

In a saucepan mix together the cream, glucose and raspberry purée. Bring to the boil stirring continuously so as not to burn the mixture. Boil for about 30 seconds, then remove from the heat and set aside to cool.

After 5 minutes, gently add the cream mixture to the melted chocolate. Stir gently until the ganache is smooth and glossy. Add the Framboise if required. Leave to set in the fridge for at least an hour.

When the ganache is set, spoon out truffle-size amounts of the mixture and roll in the raspberry powder. Store in an airtight container for up to one week. Eat and enjoy!

True ARTISANS

The only company in the UK who are wood-roasting coffee, the visionary duo behind Oxfordshire's Ue Coffee Roasters spill the beans on this unique process of creating genuine artisan coffee.

Dominic and Daniella Boyett established Ue Coffee Roasters in 2009, embarking on a journey that would lead them to become one of the most celebrated coffee roasters in the country. With over 20 years of experience in the coffee industry, Dominic's vision was to do something completely different to all the other independent coffee roasters, something truly artisan.

He's always had a reputation for thinking outside of the box and for thriving on a challenge, so he didn't pay too much attention to his industry peers who thought trying to approach the incredibly labour-intensive process of wood-roasting coffee was utterly crazy. The wood has to be as carefully selected and prepared as the coffee beans – air-dried, moisture-tested and 10-15 years old. Undeterred, Dominic and Daniella set about pioneering new developments into creating wood-roasted coffee with incredible flavour.

Starting from the basics, they had to build their own unique machines that use 100% clean hot air rather than direct heat from a gas flame for a consistent roast that is totally free from any taint of smoke. The result? Clean, sweet and full-bodied coffee, made using a process that produces very low carbon

emissions and which is 90% more sustainable than any other roastery in the country right now.

Some of the country's finest chefs are now sourcing their coffee through Ue Coffee Roasters. Chef's who have created stunning meals and matched them with the finest wines now want to make sure their guests finish their meal with a coffee that they will never forget, and one that is perfectly paired with their desserts. Working directly with farmers has allowed Dominic to really push the boundaries with what he can offer these innovative chef's – for example, he currently has a farmer in Nicaragua experimenting with papaya in the ground to yield a delightfully sweet-tasting bean.

For Dominic and Daniella, there are no limits when it comes to creating truly outstanding coffee and there are lots more exciting developments in the pipeline. This independent British business has set themselves apart from the rest, leading the way in British coffee and raising the bar for what it means to be a true artisan coffee roaster.

PROUDLY SERVING

UE COFFEE ROASTERS

TRUE ARTISAN COFFEE

HAND ROASTED IN GREAT BRITAIN

Ue Coffee Roasters'
COFFEE-RUBBED BRISKET

This was a recipe that we experienced with one of our customers and was something that we have never forgotten. We felt that this was the perfect opportunity to let everyone experience coffee, but not as a drink. Serves 3-4.

Ingredients

2 large onions, peeled and quartered

2 large white potatoes, scrubbed and cut into 2.5cm thick wedges

1 large carrot, peeled and cut into 5cm pieces

1 medium fennel bulb, cut into 4cm thick wedges

1 whole medium garlic head, unpeeled, sliced in half horizontally

2 tbsp extra-virgin olive oil

1 tbsp plus 1 tsp salt, divided

1 tsp plus ½ tsp freshly ground black pepper, divided

1 heaped tbsp Ue Coffee Roasters House Roast, ground for espresso

1 tbsp smoked cinnamon powder or regular cinnamon powder

1 tsp ground cardamom

1.8-2kg piece of well-marbled brisket, available from any good butchers

Method

Preheat the oven to 200°C/Gas Mark 6.

Place the onions, potatoes, carrot, fennel and garlic in a heavy roasting pan. Toss with the olive oil, 1 tsp salt and ½ teaspoon pepper.

In a small bowl mix the coffee, cinnamon, cardamom, remaining 1 tbsp salt, and 1 tsp pepper. Rub all over the brisket until completely covered and nestle the brisket into the vegetables to rest on the bottom of the pan.

Place in the hot oven and roast until the vegetables are lightly browned, which should take approximately 45 minutes.

Once browned, take out of the oven and cover tightly with foil. Lower the oven to 150°C/Gas Mark 2, and continue to roast until fork-tender (you should be able to insert a roasting fork in the centre and twist slightly with little resistance). Allow approximately 4½ hours for the brisket to cook, checking on it every 45 minutes. If the brisket is starting to look dry, add 2-4 tbsp water to the pan to keep it moist in-between each interval.

When the brisket is cooked, remove the roasting pan from the oven, cool to room temperature and refrigerate with the vegetables until the fat is solid; 8-24 hours.

Transfer the brisket to a board and slice across the grain. Skim and discard the fat in the roasting pan. Return the brisket slices to the roasting pan with the vegetables and cooking juices.

To serve, preheat oven to 150°C/Gas Mark 2. Transfer the roasting pan to the oven and heat the brisket until the liquid is melted and the brisket and vegetables are just warmed through; approximately 15-20 minutes.

Transfer the brisket and vegetables to a serving dish and cover tightly with foil.

Set the roasting pan over two burners on the stovetop and simmer the liquid over medium heat until thickened for 10-15 minutes.

Pour the thickened pan juices over the brisket and serve.

Hart
AND SOUL

Housed in a stunning 15th century chantry in the historic village of Fyfield is one of the finest foodie dining experiences in the county.

Just over a decade ago Kay and Mark Chandler decided to overhaul their lives in pursuit of a shared dream of opening a restaurant together. While Mark had no background in professional cooking and with Kay a banking lawyer, it seemed all of the odds were stacked against them. Fast forward 11 years and they are featured in the Good Food and Michelin Guides, have held two AA rosettes for culinary excellence for eight years and more recently were crowned Best Gastropub and Restaurant of the Year at the Oxfordshire Restaurant Awards.

What happened in between has been somewhat of a roller coaster ride, requiring an immeasurable amount of hard work, dedication and passion. Kay and Mark have lovingly restored the building to its former glory, uncovering beautiful flagstone floors, renovating the huge beams that tower three stories above the main restaurant and installing cosy log burners at either end of the building.

The garden has also been redeveloped, turning an overgrown plot in to a flourishing and bountiful kitchen garden, providing the restaurant with fresh fruit and vegetables. Much of what is grown inspires the ever-changing menu and where they can't grow it themselves, ingredients and produce are sourced locally. Mark and Kay have great contacts within the community, from local farmers who deliver fresh eggs and meat daily, to a villager who catches trout at the local reservoir in exchange for a steak dinner. Even the children get involved by foraging for wild garlic in Appleton Woods and fishing for crayfish in the summer months!

Special food evenings, such as Italian, seafood and tapas, are hugely popular and their Wednesday dinner club offers amazing value for customers who want to treat themselves mid-week. It's the customers that are at the heart of this business, some returning every week, with their regular table reserved and their favourite bottle of wine ready to pour.

Not all of their customers are what you would normally expect in a country pub, however. Prince Harry has visited on more than one occasion and they have even welcomed former American President Jimmy Carter to dine once – with all 35 of his armed bodyguards in tow!

Kay said: "We truly love what we do and every single member of our team shares our passion and dedication to bringing great food and an unforgettable experience to every customer that walks through the door."

The White Hart, Fyfield

The White Hart's
ROASTED RUMP OF COTSWOLD LAMB, BLACK OLIVE AND FETA TART WITH RATATOUILLE

Serves 6

Ingredients

For the feta tart:

250g plain flour

250g unsalted butter (125g to be cold and diced)

2 egg yolks

6 onions, finely sliced

Thyme and parsley, de-stalked, chopped

125ml double cream

50ml cold water

200g feta, diced

50g black olives, sliced

For the smoked aubergine purée:

3 aubergines

2 sprigs rosemary

4–5 garlic cloves

50ml double cream

Salt and pepper

For the ratatouille:

1 small red onion, peeled and diced

½ red, green and yellow pepper, diced

1 small courgette, diced

½ small aubergine, diced

Olive oil (good quality)

3 tomatoes, skinned, seeds removed and diced

Basil, finely chopped

For the lamb:

6 x 6-7oz lamb rumps

Thyme and rosemary sprigs

For the basil crisps:

Basil leaves and olive oil

For the garnish (optional):

Roasted red peppers quarters

Chargrilled courgette ribbons

Herb olive oil

Method

For the feta and olive tart

For the pastry, place the flour, the cold butter (125g) and a pinch of salt in a food processor. Blend until the mix resembles fine breadcrumbs. Add 1 egg yolk and the water. Pulse until the mix comes together into a dough. Roll in cling film and refrigerate for at least 1 hour. Roll out the pastry and line a 24cm, loose bottomed tin. Blind bake for 30-35 minutes at 170°C (remove the baking beans for the last 10 minutes).

For the tart filling, cook the onions, remaining butter and thyme gently until the onions are soft but not browned. Remove the mix from the pan and allow to cool. Whisk 1 egg yolk and the cream together. Add this, together with all the remaining ingredients, to the onions. Pour into the prepared tart case and bake at 180°C for 20-30 minutes until golden brown and set.

For the aubergine purée

Take two aubergines, cut in half lengthways and place a sprig of rosemary inside. Roll the two halves together in tin foil. Cut the garlic in half and roll in foil. Bake the aubergines and garlic at 200°C until very soft. Meanwhile, place the remaining aubergine directly over a gas flame or under a hot grill, until charred all over. Scoop out the soft flesh of the aubergines and garlic and place in a blender. Add the cream, salt and pepper. Blend until smooth.

For the basil crisps

Cling film a microwaveable plate. Dip the basil leaves in olive oil and place them on the plate. Place another layer of cling film tightly over the basil leaves. Microwave on full power for 3 minutes. Place the leaves on kitchen paper and reserve.

For the ratatouille

Gently sauté the onions, peppers, courgettes and aubergine in olive oil separately and then combine in a bowl. Add the raw tomato and basil. Season to taste.

For the lamb

Season the lamb generously. Preheat a pan on a medium heat. Add the thyme and rosemary to the pan and seal the lamb all over until golden brown. Place the lamb skin side down in an oven at 180°C for 10-14 minutes. Rest for 10 minutes before serving.

To serve

Carve the lamb rump into 3 slices and plate according to the photo. Roasted red pepper quarters, chargrilled courgette ribbons and a drizzle of herb oil can be added if desired.

The White Hart's
CHOCOLATE MARQUISE, LIME ICE CREAM AND SPICED CARAMEL POPCORN

Serves 4

Ingredients

For the spiced caramel:

100g caster sugar

45g unsalted butter

Seeds of 1 vanilla pod

¼ tsp ginger powder

¼ tsp cinnamon

60ml double cream

For the popcorn:

1 tbsp vegetable oil

30g popping corn

For the marquise:

100g unsalted butter

160g dark chocolate

60g icing sugar

90ml double cream

3 eggs

For the crumble:

30g unsalted butter, cold

60g caster sugar

8g cocoa powder

60g plain flour

For the lime ice cream:

100ml milk

200ml double cream

70g caster sugar

6 limes, juiced and zested

50g egg yolks

For the garnish:

1 lime

Method

For the spiced caramel

Add the sugar and a splash of water to a saucepan on a medium heat and cook until the liquid turns amber. Add the butter and spices and once melted, add the cream (be careful it does not spit). Take off the heat once it has boiled.

For the popcorn

Heat the oil in a saucepan with a lid on a medium heat. Add the corn and place the lid on. Remove from the heat once the popping has stopped. Cover the popcorn in half of the caramel sauce and bake for 10 minutes at 120°C until crispy.

For the marquise

Melt the butter, chocolate and half the icing sugar over a bain-marie. Meanwhile, whip the cream into soft peaks. Whisk in the egg whites and remaining icing sugar to form soft peaks again. Once the chocolate mix is melted, remove from the heat and beat in the egg yolks. Fold in a third of the cream mix. Repeat this step until everything is incorporated. Then pipe into moulds (we use cylinders but any shape can be used) and refrigerate.

For the crumble

In a food processor, mix everything for 15 seconds, then bake for 10-12 minutes at 180°C.

For the lime ice cream

Add the milk, cream, sugar and lime juice to a pan and bring to the boil. Pour this mix over the egg yolks in a bowl, stirring all the time. Return to the pan and cook to 82°C (until it starts to thicken). Leave to cool. Add the lime zest and churn in an ice cream machine.

To serve

Sprinkle the crumble and the zest of a lime on the plate and then arrange the marquise and ice cream according to the photo along with the popcorn.

Food from THE HART

Nestled in the historic village of Minster Lovell, The White Hart is a traditional family-run pub with a beautiful country dining room and the friendliest service in Oxfordshire.

Since Brian and Amanda Barker took over the attractive coaching inn in 2014, The White Hart has seen a transformation that has put it back at the heart of its community in rural Oxfordshire. With a fantastic team, a talented head chef and not forgetting Rosaline the resident ghost, Brian and Amanda have seen The White Hart quickly become a cherished part of Minster Lovell life.

Head chef Thomas Curtis is the man behind the menu. The country-style dining room provides a different ambience to the traditional bar area of the pub – both equally warm and inviting, but with the pub retaining the 'proper pub feel' and the dining room offering a touch of elegance for enjoying Tom's acclaimed cooking. Whichever area you are sitting in, the family feel and personal touch permeates every aspect of the service.

Thomas's menu is varied and creative, changing regularly depending on what ingredients are available to him locally and seasonally. Although due to public demand, his white chocolate and milky way cheesecake has become a permanent fixture. His Sunday roasts have also reached legendary status in the area and they can be booked up on Sundays for weeks in advance.

Named 'Best Traditional Pub' at the Oxfordshire Restaurant Awards in 2015 and with a TripAdvisor Certificate of Excellence already under their belt, The White Hart has been going from strength to strength. It's all thanks to teamwork – something The White Hart is really proud of. From the kitchen staff to the bartenders, everybody has a welcoming smile and a commitment to excellence.

There is always something a little bit different happening at The White Hart, and we're not just talking about mysterious happenings attributed to the resident ghost… the annual magic night hosted by a world-class local magician proved immensely popular, as did Thomas's accompanying themed menu. With an enthusiastic team and plenty of creativity in the kitchen, there are sure to be more unique events planned for the future.

The White Hart

PASSION FRUIT PANNA COTTA, BLACK TREACLE BANANA CAKE, TOASTED COCONUT, RASPBERRIES AND ROSE PETALS

A beautiful finish to many a meal at The White Hart. Serves 6

Ingredients

For the panna cotta:

500ml whole milk

100ml evaporated milk

5 tsp caster sugar

1 vanilla pod

4 gelatine leaves

3 passion fruits

For the black treacle banana cake:

100g softened unsalted butter

100g caster sugar

30ml dark rum

2 eggs

100g plain flour

1 tsp baking powder

2 ripe bananas

8 tbsp black treacle

4 tbsp water

For the garnish:

30 fresh raspberries

6 tsp toasted desiccated coconut

1 tsp dried rose petals

Method

In a heavy-based saucepan add the whole milk, evaporated milk and caster sugar. Split the vanilla pod and scrape the seeds into the milk and pop in the pod as well. Stir over a medium heat to gently bring the mix to a simmer. Take off of the heat and leave it to infuse for 10-15 minutes.

Soak the gelatine leaves in cold water for 5 minutes, squeeze gently to get rid of the excess water and whisk into the milk mixture.

Halve each passion fruit and divide the fruit between 6 small (100ml) pudding moulds or ramekins lined with cling film.

Strain the panna cotta mix into a pouring jug and skim off any froth to leave a clean smooth mixture. Divide this mixture between the moulds or ramekins and leave to set in a fridge for at least 4 hours.

Preheat the oven to 160°C. Grease and line a 25cm x 20cm x 5cm baking tray with parchment paper.

Beat together the softened butter, caster sugar and rum until pale and airy. Add the eggs and beat until well combined. Sift in the flour and baking powder and fold in gently.

In a food processor, blend the bananas and 4 tbsp of the black treacle. Fold this into your cake batter. Transfer the mix to your greased and lined baking tray. Cook on the middle shelf in the oven for 20 minutes, until a cocktail stick, inserted into the centre, comes out clean. Allow to cool on a rack. Cut into small cubes and transfer to a bowl or tub. Warm the remaining treacle in a pan with 4 tbsp of water to make a syrup. Drizzle over the cut cake and give it a gentle mix.

To plate it up, bring a pan of water to the boil (you want just enough water to come about three-quarters of the way up the panna cotta moulds). Very carefully place each mould in the water for about 10 seconds. Quickly flip the mould onto the centre of your serving dish and persuade it out with a little squeeze and wiggle. If using ramekins lined with cling film, very gently remove the panna cotta's and unwrap on the serving dishes.

Place five pieces of the banana cake around the panna cotta with five raspberries between. Sprinkle over the toasted coconut and a few rose petals. Enjoy.

It's rabbit
SEASON

With executive chef Tim Allen at the helm, The Wild Rabbit continues to champion British producers both locally and from further afield, to create a menu using quality, artisanal and where possible organic produce.

An impressive career that includes four years at Launceston Place in Kensington as chef patron (where the restaurant gained a Michelin star and 4 AA Rosettes) and before that seven years at the two Michelin-starred Whatley Manor with Martin Burge has provided Tim with a wealth of fine dining experience. This, combined with a strong ethos that favours seasonal quality ingredients, has made Tim and The Wild Rabbit the perfect match.

A re-invention of the traditional English inn, the eighteenth century Wild Rabbit combines stripped back walls, open fires and hand crafted furniture with excellent hospitality. Their 12 stunning rooms combined with food and drink that celebrates independent producers makes this a winning formula.

Before you even get to the dining room you'll find local cask ales on the bar, a variety of artisan beers and a wine list that supports small independent vineyards.

The menu also reflects this philosophy, using organic ingredients from the nearby Daylesford farm, alongside quality artisanal products from around the world and foraged ingredients when the season dictates. For instance, a yield of crayfish from the river Evenlode are incorporated into the menu with a slow-cooked pheasant egg and elderberries

from the surrounding hedgerows which are pickled in white balsamic vinegar and served with hare. Game also features prominently in the autumn, as part of a naturally changing menu that showcases ingredients in their absolute prime.

The rest of the offering combines everything from Wootton Estate lamb with confit tomatoes, English asparagus and Parmesan bon bon, to hand-lined cod, pure parsley, moules marinière and matchstick potatoes. They also boast charcoal cooked rib eye and sirloin on the bone, both of which are dry aged for forty days, and from mature herds.

For a more private affair, The Chicken Shed, a self-contained outbuilding, serves as the perfect setting for private dinners or parties. The contemporary room is decorated simply with seasonal floral touches to show off the original exposed beams, stone walls and a wood fired oven.

Whether you're popping in for a tipple from a local brewery to go with a light lunch, or staying the whole weekend and sampling the region's finest from the à la carte, you'll be sure to receive a plateful of cuisine that is truly unique to Oxfordshire.

The Wild Rabbit

QUAIL

Serves 4

Ingredients

4 whole quail

Morteau sausage, thinly sliced

For the eggs:

4 quail eggs

5 tbsp plain flour, sifted and seasoned

1 egg, beaten for dipping

150g panko breadcrumbs

Oil, for deep frying

For the smoked shallot purée:

12 banana shallots, skin on

160ml double cream

1 tsp salt

Pinch of ground white pepper

2 tsp lemon juice

For the verjus jelly:

500ml verjus

70g sugar

1 tsp salt

100ml red grape juice

30g elastic (gelling agent available online)

For the glazed raisins:

100g raisins

400ml grape juice

For the shallot rings:

8 shallots, peeled and sliced

4 tbsp plain flour

1 tsp salt

For the garnish:

4 gem lettuce hearts, charred

Method

For the quail
Preheat the oven to 180°C.

To cook the quail, heat two tablespoons of oil in a hot ovenproof frying pan.

Pan-roast the whole quail for 1 minute 30 seconds on its breast, then cook on the other breast for another 1 minute 30 seconds. Then roast on the crown for a further 1 minute 30 seconds.

Place in a medium oven for 6 minutes, remove and rest for a further 6 minutes.

For the quail eggs
Boil the eggs in their shells for 1 minute and 20 seconds then plunge into ice water. When cold, carefully peel.

Lightly coat each egg in the flour, the beaten egg then the breadcrumbs. Lightly shape by hand.

To cook, deep fry for 1 minute and a half at 180°C.

For the shallot purée
Remove any excess paper and root from the shallots. Score the shallot 5 times taking care not to cut too far down into the flesh. Wrap the shallots in tin foil to make a papillote. Cook on a medium heat for 1 hour to 1 hour 25 minutes.

When the shallots are cooked remove from the papillote and peel whilst warm, taking care not to waste any flesh. Place the warm shallot halves on a cooling rack ready to smoke.

Leave to smoke for 30 minutes (you can get home smokers from any good online retailer) and then switch off and leave for 20 minutes.

Boil the double cream and reduce to 120ml. Blitz the shallots with the cream and seasoning for 8 minutes until smooth. Pass over ice and place in the freezer.

For the verjus jelly
Spray a large flat tray with pastry oil.

In a saucepan over a medium to high heat reduce the verjus by about a fifth.

Blend in all of the remaining ingredients. Cook out at 200°C while mixing.

Be aware that the elastic gelling agent becomes active at 85°C and must be cooked out.

Skim lightly as foam appears. You will notice a colour change and a clear liquid forming.

Working quickly, pour into a cling film lined tray, let it set at room temperature then refrigerate until needed.

For the glazed raisins
In a saucepan add the grape juice and raisins and bring to a boil.

Reduce the heat to a gentle simmer, cover the pan with cling film and cook on a gentle heat for 2 hours.

Remove the cling film and reduce the grape juice to a sticky and syrupy consistency being careful not to caramelise.

For the shallot rings
Season the flour.

Slice the shallots into rings, dredge in seasoned flour and deep fry until golden.

To serve
Remove the breasts from the quail and crisp the skin in a frying pan, then add to the plate.

Pour a little verjus on each quail breast.

Add the shallot purée to the plate, and top with the crisp shallot rings.

Place around 3 slices of Morteau sausage on each plate.

Add the deep-fried quail eggs.

Char the gem lettuce hearts with a blow torch, or under a hot grill and top with a disc of verjus jelly.

The Wild Rabbit

WHITE CHOCOLATE SPHERE, CARAMELISED CHOCOLATE, YORKSHIRE RHUBARB AND STRAWBERRIES

There are a few techniques in this dish but the end result
is well-worth the effort. Serves 6

Ingredients

8 large strawberries, lightly washed,
leaves and stem removed

For the caramelised white chocolate:

480g white chocolate

**For the caramelised white chocolate
sorbet:**

370g white chocolate, caramelised
above

100g glucose

900ml water

1 tsp salt

2 tbsp sugar

20g prosorbet (available to buy
online)

100g milk powder

For the white chocolate mousse:

480g white chocolate

80g icing sugar

4 egg yolks

120g whipping cream

12g gelatine

800g whipping cream

For the rhubarb sorbet:

450ml rhubarb syrup

70ml rhubarb purée

40ml rhubarb juice

10g prosorbet

For the poached rhubarb:

2 large sticks of rhubarb, poached

200g sugar

200ml water

200ml grenadine

Method

For the caramelised white chocolate

Gently melt the chocolate in a pan, keep on the heat until the sugars caramelise and turn
the chocolate a light golden brown. Try different levels of caramelisation to see what you
prefer.

For the white chocolate sorbet

Heat the glucose, water, sugar, and salt together in a pan.

When boiled, hand-blend with the chocolate, milk powder and prosorbet.

Churn whilst hot, otherwise the sorbet will separate and become lumpy.

For the white chocolate mousse

Set up the bain-marie and melt the chocolate. Mix the icing sugar and egg yolks together
then add the egg yolks to the melted chocolate. Dissolve the gelatine with 120g of boiled
cream. Add the hot cream to the above chocolate and mix to form a smooth ganache.
Allow to cool down before folding in the whipped cream. This will make more than you
need but the rest can go in the fridge/freezer to eat later!

For the rhubarb sorbet

Blend all of the ingredients together and leave to macerate for 3 hours. Churn the sorbet.

For the poached rhubarb

Add the sugar, water and grenadine to a saucepan and dissolve on a low heat.

Trim and peel the rhubarb and cut into 2 inch pieces.

Poach in the syrup until tender.

To plate

Arrange on the plate in a way you are happy with, or copy the picture opposite, there is no
right or wrong way.

The DIRECTORY

These great businesses have supported the making of this book; please support and enjoy them.

The Baskerville
7 Station Road
Lower Shiplake
Henley-on-Thames
Oxfordshire RG9 3NY
Telephone: 01189 403332
Website: www.thebaskerville.com
A perfect blend of traditional village pub, first class restaurant where food really does matter and superb accommodation.

Blue Tin Produce
Keepers Cottage
Garsons Farm
Ipsden OX10 6QU
Telephone: 01491 681145
Website: www.bluetinproduce.co.uk
Rare breed meats reared using traditional methods in a beautiful Oxfordshire setting, with on-site farm shop.

Chadlington Quality Foods
The Gables
West End, Chadlington
Chipping Norton
Oxfordshire OX7 3NJ
Telephone: 01608 676675
Website: www.chadlingtonqualityfoods.com
The quintessential village store, selling a range of delicious homemade products that have been created in our own kitchen.

The Cherry Tree Inn
Main Street
Stoke Row
Henley-on-Thames
Oxfordshire
RG9 5QA
Telephone: 01491 680 430
Website: www.thecherrytreeinn.co.uk
Situated in a 'designated area of outstanding natural beauty', this 18th century pub with four barn conversion rooms offers great food, locally sourced, freshly cooked and with innovative style.

Cogges Kitchen
Cogges Manor Farm,
Church Lane,
Witney OX28 3LA
Telephone: 01993 772602
Website: www.cogges.org.uk
Enjoy a daily changing menu inspired by the Cogges walled garden and orchard in the beautiful old milking parlour in the grounds of Cogges Manor Farm.

Cotswold Baking Ltd
Unit A3
Heath Farm
Swerford OX7 4BN
Website: www.cotswoldbaking.co.uk
Producer of hand-crafted artisan cakes and patisserie.

The Cotswold Plough Hotel & Restaurant – The Cotswold Gin Pantry
Bourton Rd,
Clanfield,
Bampton OX18 2RB
Telephone: 01367 810222
Website: www.cotswoldsploughhotel.com
Hotel and restaurant with a bespoke Gin Pantry, offering hundreds of different gins to try as well as events like tastings, blending, 'afternoon G&T' and more.

The Crooked Billet
Newlands Lane,
Stoke Row,
Henley-on-Thames,
Oxon
RG9 5PU
Telephone: 01491 681048
Website: www.thecrookedbillet.co.uk
Crowned the UK's first gastropub, The Crooked Billet combines rustic charm with a varied daily changing menu and special local events.

Delicacy Deli and Coffee Shop
2 Middle Row
Chipping Norton
Oxon OX7 5NH
Telephone: 01608 642843
Website: www.delicacy.org.uk
A beautiful deli and coffee shop in the heart of the Cotswolds, offering a huge range of tasty products – feast your eyes!

Eynsham Cellars
43 Mill Street
Eynsham
Witney OX29 4JX
Telephone: 01865 884405
Website: www.eynshamcellars.com
Friendly, independent wine merchant offering wines, beers and spirits, alongside running tasting events and pop-up wine bars. Open late 7 days a week!

Fingers and Forks
Bix Manor
Bix, Henley-On-Thames
Oxfordshire RG9 4RS
Telephone: 01491 877402
Website: www.fingersandforks.co.uk
Professional caterers offering top quality bespoke catering services with superb food and excellent service, for groups large and small.

Gabriel Machin
7 Market Place
Henley-on-Thames
Oxon RG9 2AA
Telephone: 01491 574377
Website: www.gabrielmachin.co.uk
Henley's favourite butcher since 1910.

Hand-crafted cultured butter by Grant Harrington
Ampersand
Lords Farm
Oxfordshire
Twitter/Instagram: @butterculture
culturedgrant@gmail.com
Restaurant supplier and butter specialist.

House of Jacob
Jacobs and Field
15 Old High Street,
Headington,
Oxford OX3 9HP
Telephone: 01865766990
Website: www.jacobsandfield.com
The House of Jacob incorporates four different venues, from the bustling deli Jacobs and Field to Jacobs Chop House, offering traditionally cooked meats washed down with real ales and fine wines. They also have two gastropubs, The Woodstock Arms and Jacobs Inn, whose seasonal menus reflect the best of local produce.

Jacobs Chop House
3, Manor Buildings,
Osler Road,
Oxford OX3 7RA
Telephone: 01865 764486
Website: www.jacobschophouse.com
The Woodstock Arms
6-8 Market Street,
Woodstock,
Oxford OX20 1SX
Telephone: 01993 811251
Website: www.thewoodstockarms.com
Jacobs Inn
130 Godstow Road,
Wolvercote,
Oxford OX2 8PG
Telephone: 01865 514333
Website: www.jacobs-inn.com

The Kitchen Farnborough
Main Street,
Farnborough,
Nr. Banbury OX17 1DZ
Telephone: 01295 690615
Website: www.thekitchenfarnborough.co.uk
Great quality food from The Kitchen garden and a few local heroes, freshly made in a stunning rural location.

Miller of Mansfield
High St,
Goring,
Reading RG8 9AW
Telephone: 01491 872829
Website: www.millerofmansfield.com
With individually designed rooms, a menu boasting food from the freshest seasonal British ingredients, a well-chosen wine list, cocktails and proper pints, the Miller of Mansfield has it all under one roof.

The Muddy Duck
Main St, Hethe
Nr Bicester
Oxfordshire OX27 8ES
Telephone: 01869 278099
Website: www.themuddyduckpub.
co.uk
*Traditional service with tomorrow's food
– right up your rural street!*

Natural Bread Company
29 Little Clarendon Street
Oxford OX1 2HU
Telephone: 01865 302996
Website: www.naturalbreadcompany.
co.uk
*An independent, family-run artisan
bakery with café and bread shops in
Oxford, Woodstock and Eynsham.*

The Nut Tree Inn
Main Street
Murcott
Oxfordshire OX5 2RE
Telephone: 01865 331253
Website: www.nuttreeinn.co.uk
*A local pub serving the community as
well as a Michelin-starred destination
restaurant.*

The Oxford Arms
Troy Lane, Kirtlington
Oxfordshire OX5 3HA
Telephone: 01869 350208
Website: www.oxford-arms.co.uk
*An award-winning dining pub in
Oxfordshire, situated in a wonderful
19th-century building steeped in history.*

The Oxford Cheese Company Ltd
17 Covered Market
Oxford
OX1 3DU
Telephone: 01844 338055
or 01865 721420
Website: www.oxfordfinefood.com
and www.oxfordcheese.co.uk
*Purveyors of fine cheese and home of the
famous Oxford Blue cheese.*

The Oxford Kitchen
215 Banbury Road
Summertown
Oxford OX2 7HQ
Telephone: 01865 511 149
Website: www.theoxfordkitchen.co.uk
*Award-winning relaxed fine dining in
Summertown, Oxford.*

Pierreponts Café
1 High Street
Goring-on-Thames
Oxfordshire
RG8 9AB
Telephone: 01491 874464
Website: www.pierreponts.co.uk
*Charming café offering breakfast, brunch,
lunch and afternoon tea, with menus and
specials ranging from simple to indulgent.
Relaxed dinners and fine wine on Friday
evenings from 6pm.*

Plantation Chocolates
by Vivien Shelton
Telephone: 07900 261517
Website: www.plantationchocolates.
co.uk
Email: vivien@plantationchocolates.
co.uk/vivienshelton@mac.com
*An award-winning, fine chocolate
company based in Oxford.*

The Pointer
27 Church St
Brill
Bucks HP18 9RT
Telephone: 01844 238339
Website: www.thepointerbrill.co.uk
*A country pub, restaurant and butchers
with its own farm. Serving fantastic,
simple, seasonal and thoroughly delicious
food and drink to all who cross its
threshold.*

The Quince Tree
River & Rowing Museum,
Henley-on-Thames RG9 1BF
Telephone: 01491 579215
Email: home@thequincetree.com
*The Quince Tree can be found in the heart
of Henley-on-Thames at the River &
Rowing Museum as well as at multi-
award-winning Clifton Nurseries -
London's oldest garden centre.*

The Quince Tree
Clifton Nurseries
5a Clifton Villas,
London W9 2PH
Telephone: 020 7432 1867
Website: www.thequincetree.com
*Offering a selection of handmade
pâtisserie, savoury treats and daily
specials, as well as picnic hampers and
catering for private events.*

Ross & Ross Food Ltd
10 Worcester Road Trading Estate
Chipping Norton
Oxfordshire OX7 5XW
Telephone: 01608 645503
Website: www.rossandrossfood.co.uk
*Event and wedding caterers and
handmade British food gifts.*

Sudbury House
Restaurant 56 and Magnolia
Brasserie
56 London Street, Faringdon
Oxfordshire SN7 7AA
Telephone: 01367 241272
Website: www.sudburyhouse.co.uk
*Sudbury House provides a mix of old
and new – a contemporary 50-bedroom
hotel, home to the Magnolia Brasserie, a
relaxed informal restaurant, and a Grade
II-listed building, proudly presenting
Restaurant 56, our 3 AA rosette fine-
dining restaurant.*

Tutu Delicious Chocolate
26-30 High Street
Watlington
Oxfordshire OX49 5PY
Telephone: 01491 612462
Website: www.tutudelicious.co.uk
*We are a small independent, artisan
chocolate company producing award
winning, exquisite chocolates in
Watlington, Oxfordshire.*

Ue Coffee Roasters Ltd
11a–11b Windrush Ind. Park
Linkwood Road, Witney
Oxfordshire OX29 7HA
Telephone: 01993 706767
Website: www.uecoffeeroasters.com
*Supporting home baristas and industry
front-runners, with the UK's first and
only artisan hand-crafted wood-roasted
coffees.*

The White Hart at Fyfield
Main Road,
Fyfield,
Abingdon OX13 5LW
Telephone: 01865 390585
Website: www.whitehart-fyfield.com
*Under the eaves of a 15th century
chantry house, enjoy award-winning
food, fine wines and local real ales.*

The White Hart at Minster
Burford Road, Minster Lovell
Witney OX29 0RA
Telephone: 01993 778629
Website: www.thewhitehartminster.
co.uk
*An award-winning country pub serving
great food and drink.*

The Wild Rabbit
Church Street,
Kingham,
Oxfordshire OX7 6YA
Telephone: 01608 658389
Website: www.thewildrabbit.co.uk
*The Wild Rabbit lies in the heart of
the Cotswolds, offering a contemporary
take on the traditional inn, with twelve
beautiful rooms and a seasonal menu
from executive chef Tim Allen.*

Other titles in the 'Get Stuck In' series

The Sheffield Cook Book
features Baldwin's Omega,
Nonna's, Ashoka, Cubana,
Peppercorn and lots more.
978-0-9928981-0-6

The Nottingham Cook Book
features Sat Bains with
Rooms, World Service, Harts,
Escabeche and lots more.
978-0-9928981-5-1

The Derbyshire Cook Book
features Chatsworth
Estate, Fischer's of Baslow,
Thornbridge Brewery and lots
more.
978-0-9928981-7-5

The Cambridgeshire Cook Book
features Daniel Clifford of
Midsummer House, The Pint
Shop, Gog Magog Hills, Clare
College and lots more.
978-0-9928981-9-9

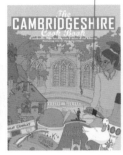

The Suffolk Cook Book
features Jimmy Doherty of
Jimmy's Farm, Gressingham
Duck and lots more.
978-1-910863-02-2

The Manchester Cook Book
features Aiden Byrne, Simon
Rogan, Harvey Nichols and
lots more.
978-1-910863-01-5

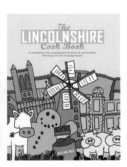

The Lincolnshire Cook Book
features Colin McGurran of
Winteringham Fields,
TV chef Rachel Green,
San Pietro and lots more.
978-1-910863-05-3

The Newcastle Cook Book
features David Coulson
of Peace & Loaf, Bealim
House, Grainger Market,
Quilliam Brothers and lots
more.
978-1-910863-04-6

The Cheshire Cook Book
features Simon Radley of
The Chester Grosvenor, The
Chef's Table, Great North
Pie Co., Harthill Cookery
School and lots more.
978-1-910863-07-7

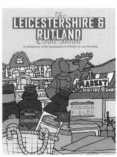

**The Leicestershire & Rutland
Cook Book** features Tim Hart
of Hambleton Hall, John's
House, Farndon Fields,
Leicester Market, Walter
Smith and lots more.
978-0-9928981-8-2

*All books in this series are available from Waterstones,
Amazon and independent bookshops.*

FIND OUT MORE ABOUT US AT WWW.MEZEPUBLISHING.CO.UK